TOYAGER
A Toy Piano Method

Elizabeth A. Baker

Edited By: Fofi Panagiotouros
Photography By: Fofi Panagiotouros
Cover Art By: Susan Dickson-Nadeau

FIRST EDITION

© 2016 Elizabeth Ann Baker
Saint Petersburg, Florida 33712
All rights reserved. No part of this book may be reproduced,
stored in a retrieval system, or transcribed, in any form or
by any means, electronic, mechanical, photocopying, recording,
or otherwise, without the express written permission of the author
or the publisher.

ISBN-13: 978-0692662014 (Elizabeth A. Baker)
ISBN-10: 0692662014

Printed in the United States of America

About the author

Celebrated for her "terrifying dynamic range," cleanliness of sound, as well as unique sensitivity and ability to sculpt her performance for the acoustics of a space, Elizabeth A. Baker is a dramatic performer with an honest, near psychic connection to the music, which resounds with audiences of all ages and musical backgrounds. As a composer, her understanding of sonic space pairs with a unique eclectic voice, making for a spatial and auditory experience of music. As a pianist, Baker has studied with Steinway Artist Dr. Luis Sanchez and Jeff Donovick of St. Petersburg College and enjoys an active concert career with performances across the nation. Her advisors have included composer and choral director Dr. Vernon Taranto. Emmy-award winning composer Larry Groupé has referred to her works as "Perfect." Elizabeth's works have been featured by  Composers Circle, FIVE by FIVE, TEDxYouthTampaBay, Tampa Mini Makers Faire, Orlando Mini Makers Faire, as well as at the 2014 Electronic Music Midwest Festival and the 19th International Festival of Women Composers. In 2015 she received an Individual Artist Grant from the Saint Petersburg Arts Alliance and the City of Saint Petersburg, Florida to create and present an original sound installation In Our Own Words: A Sonic Memory Quilt, which told the stories of various African-Americans in a fresh avant-garde manner, framed by evolving drones and a four-hour live performance by Elizabeth. In addition to her work as a performer-composer, Elizabeth has extensive technical training in the recording arts, live sound reinforcement, and was the recipient of the 2012 Best Production Award in Music Technology III at St. Petersburg College, where she studied closely under mastering engineer Dave Greenberg.

Combining her love of technology and keyboard instruments, Elizabeth has recently embarked on a mission to promote works for toy piano and electronics, using a setup that combines microphones, which she has built by hand. Her original works have been hailed by the Orlando Weekly as "a sterling testimonial to her artistry that proves she's not just an expert in the toy piano field but a pioneer." Elizabeth is co-founder of the innovative toy piano and electronics duo Toyeurism along with Robert Fleitz. In Fall 2015, Schoenhut Piano Company added Elizabeth A. Baker to their official artist roster. A sensitive improviser, with experience in a wide array of genres, Elizabeth is a frequent collaborator for ensembles across Florida including Jim Ivy's Tangled Bell Ensemble. She has also shared the stage with legendary trombonist and free jazz interpreter Steve Swell.

Elizabeth is dedicated to promoting new music and has a passion for making rare concert works accessible to the general public. Her preferred concert presentation method engages the audience by breaking the fourth wall and asking them to consider the tiniest elements of the composition and reminding them that there is no such thing as an incorrect interpretation of a work. She firmly believes that every person will encounter music in a unique manner because each person comes from a different set of cultural norms, life experiences, and even the way they physically hear can be a factor to consider when seeking to relate with a work.

Elizabeth is Founder and Executive Director of The New Music Conflagration, Inc., a not-for-profit corporation founded in the State of Florida to promote the work of contemporary composers and musicians. She is also, Co-Founder of the Florida International Toy Piano Festival. **elizabethabaker.com**

About the editor

Fofi Panagiotouros is a music educator, and collaborative pianist currently residing in the Tampa Bay Area. Panagiotouros is a graduate of Florida Southern College, where her studies were concentrated on music education and psychology. She has studied piano with Rita Fandrich, Paula Parsché, and Steinway Artist Dr. Luis Sanchez. Panagiotouros currently studies with internationally acclaimed concert pianist and pedagogue Dr. Duncan MacMillan. She is presently, an elementary music educator for Pinellas County Schools in Florida and a teacher for the inaugural Fourth-and-Fifth-Grade Band Instrumental Program (FBI) in Seminole, Florida. Panagiotouros has worked with several academic ensembles across the county, through her directing and coaching those groups and soloists went on to receive top ratings in both district as well as state competitions. Panagiotouros is also, heavily involved with private music education, in addition to her work as a piano instructor for her own studio and other studios, she has worked as a woodwind teacher in the Tampa Bay area. As a performer, she maintains an active schedule as an accompanist and collaborative pianist. Panagiotouros is Director of Community Outreach for The New Music Conflagration, Inc., a 501(c)(3) nonprofit organization, and 509(a)(2) public charity, which promotes contemporary concert music and educates the community about modern music. As Director of Community Outreach, Panagiotouros is responsible for student scholarships, overseeing community volunteers, and managing donations from small business sponsors, in addition to grant writing and marinating relationships with corporate sponsors.

CONTENTS

UNDERSTANDING THE TOY PIANO

CHAPTER ONE	INTRODUCTION	3
CHAPTER TWO	COMPOSERS & WRITING FOR TOY PIANO	7
CHAPTER THREE	NOTABLE PLAYERS	11
CHAPTER FOUR	MODERN PRODUCTION TOY PIANO MODELS	13
CHAPTER FIVE	PRINCIPLES OF TECHNIQUE	14

UNDERSTANDING MUSIC NOTATION

CHAPTER SIX	COMMON QUESTIONS	25
CHAPTER SEVEN	COMMON NOTATION & SYMBOLS	27
CHAPTER EIGHT	RHYTHM STUDIES	35
CHAPTER NINE	INTERVALS	38
CHAPTER TEN	KEY SIGNATURES	41
CHAPTER ELEVEN	SCALES	43
CHAPTER TWELVE	CHORDS	44
CHAPTER THIRTEEN	TRANSPOSITION	46

PRACTICE AND PERFORMANCE

CHAPTER FOURTEEN	PRACTICE	51
CHAPTER FIFTEEN	IMPROVISATION	54

APPENDICES

CIRCLE OF FIFTHS	61
DIATONIC CHORD CHART	62
DYNAMICS CHART	63
FINGERING CHART	64
KEY SIGNATURE CHART	65
KEYBOARD DIAGRAM	66
RHYTHM CHART	67
TEMPO CHART	68
TREBLE CLEF & STAFF	69

GLOSSARY   71

WRITTEN EXERCISES   77

PLAYING EXERCISES

RHYTHM STUDIES	115
INTERVALS	125
SCALES	133
PATTERNS	145
SOLO WORKS	151
IMPROVISATION	171

PRACTICE PLANNER   179

UNDERSTANDING THE TOY PIANO

CHAPTER ONE
INTRODUCTION

Albert Schoenhut

In 1872 and in his twenties Albert Schoenhut started the A. Schoenhut Co. which would later become known as the Schoenhut Piano Company. Schoenhut was born into a toy-making family, and showed an interest in building toy pianos from an early age. Schoenhut moved from his native homeland of Germany to the United States of America in 1866 when he was hired by John Dahl, a buyer for Wanamaker's department store in Philadelphia, to repair glass parts on German toy pianos. After several years in service at the department store, Schoenhut left to pursue his own toy instrument company, which produced toy pianos as well as ukulele-banjos, xylophones, and glockenspiels. At one point, the company grew so large that it branched out into circus figures, dolls, and other toys. Upon Schoenhut's death in 1912, he had built a toy empire that was larger than any in the United States and was the first company to export toys to Germany. Today's owners of the Schoenhut Piano Company are Len and Renee Trinca of St. Augustine Beach, Florida, who acquired ownership of the company in 1996. Schoenhut introduced the concept of using graduated metal bars, instead of the breakage prone glass bars that were common to toy pianos of the time. The Trincas have continued this tradition of innovation and in 2016 unveiled a new digital toy piano model, which boasts a host of learning features for children as well as recording capabilities to foster their creative impulse.

Why toy piano?

A common question asked during interviews of toy piano performers and composers, is why do you play on/write for toy piano. While there are many unique answers the common thread running through each response is that the toy piano causes one to think about music in a different manner. For some it evokes a child-like sense of whimsy, for others it is about the challenge of writing for an instrument with a limited pitch range, others just like the way it sounds in all of it's non-standard tuning glory.

There has been a revival of toy piano on the concert stage and recordings of recent years, but it has a rich history of use by composers within an ensemble settings such as George Crumb's master work, *Ancient Voices of Children*, as well as a solo performance as in John Cage's *Suite for Toy Piano* composed during his time at Black Mountain College in 1948. Today, toy piano virtuoso and the first woman to receive a doctorate from the prestigious Juilliard School in New York City, Margret Lang Tan champions the case for toy piano as a concert instrument. Her whimsical concerts have moved the hearts and minds of skeptics that believe the toy piano does not have the substance to be considered a serious concert instrument. Toy piano festivals promoting the creation of new works for the instrument have popped up across the continental United States in California, New York, and Florida. There are groups of composers dedicated to the creation of new concert works for toy instruments across the globe including Toy Piano Composers started by Monica Pearse in Canada. Commercial music acts have used toy piano in the studio for many years, most notably Australian singer-songwriter Ben Lee received critical acclaim for his 2005 album *Awake is the New Sleep*, which prominently featured toy piano on the track *Catch My Disease*. Other instances of commercial music usage of toy piano can be found on albums from popular artists including: Tom Waits, Clap Your Hands Say Yeah, The Dresden Dolls, Lenny Kravitz, and Radiohead.

While the toy piano has a promising future in the world of concert music, it still remains a valuable teaching instrument for those wishing to learn the basics of piano technique and musical language. It is a perfect beginning instrument for small children because it comfortably fits growing hands while still being of comfortable size for adults to demonstrate. Furthermore, the durability of toy piano construction means that the average four-year-old can give the piano a playful beating and still have a usable instrument at the end.

Sound Production

Toy pianos employ a similar, though far less complex, mechanism of sound production to their 88-key full-sized cousins. In a large piano, sound is produced when a felt hammer, which strikes strings from underneath causing them to vibrate against a board that amplifies the sound of the vibrating strings. Playing any musical instrument requires the performer to transfer energy from their body to an inanimate object. In sharing our life force with an instrument we project our spirit into the sounds it create and this is the integral essence needed to present a truly artistic performance. To understand the transfer of energy from the pianist to the physical instrument, one must begin to picture the key mechanism as a children's playground teeter-totter. The transfer of weight from a key to the hammer along a fulcrum is akin to the rise-and-fall of the teeter-totter. Traditional piano mechanisms also, employ a damper system, which stops the strings from vibrating when the keys are not in play, the damper mechanism can be altered in real-time to prolong the sustain of the strings. Playing mechanisms on real pianos are made from materials including: metal, wood, and felt, the result is a heavy yet, very responsive instrument. The developing hands of children, first attempting to play a full-sized piano often find difficulty in depressing the keys, partially because they lack the weight to make the other end of the keyboard teeter-totter go up. The solution for modern toy pianos has been the implementation of a lightweight plastic hammer mechanism.

PLASTIC HAMMER IN MOTION INSIDE 25-KEY TABLETOP MODEL

PLASTIC HAMMER STRIKING TINE INSIDE 25-KEY TABLETOP MODEL

FOR VIDEO OF THE INNER WORKINGS OF THE KEYBOARD MECHANISM, PLEASE VISIT THE TOYAGER YOUTUBE CHANNEL.

Due to the fact that traditional pianos have a soundboard over which strings are fixed, in conjunction with the complex system of moving parts necessary to produce sound; full-sized pianos are essentially machines, which require regular maintenance. Just as a car needs regular oil changes, tune-ups, and tires; full-sized pianos demand regular tunings, adjustments to the playing mechanism, and after awhile of playing new felt for their hammers. A toy piano uses a series of pitched graduated metal bars called **tines**, instead of strings. While strings can stretch, solid metal is harder to fine tune and for this reason, the toy piano is difficult to tune. On the positive side, solid metal bars cause each instrument develops a unique signature sound as it ages. People with "perfect pitch" who are accustomed to the Western **equal temperament** tuning system centered about concert pitch (A-440 for America) may find the toy piano jarring because it stays "in tune" with itself but does not tune to concert pitch. The metal tines also, give the toy piano a music box **timbre** (distinctive sound character), which over prolonged sessions of solo play may be perceived as quite harsh to some listeners.

For those who are unfamiliar with musical definitions, a detailed introduction to music notation and harmony is located later in this book.

Typical ranges

Toy pianos come in a variety of sizes but the most common in production today are 18-keys, 25-keys, 30-keys, and 37-keys. These key numbers correspond with the number of octaves that the instrument has:

- 18-keys = 1.5 octaves
- 25-key = 2 octaves
- 30-key = 2.5 octaves
- 37-key = 3 octaves

This book is written exclusively for the Schoenhut Piano Company My First Piano II, a 25-key tabletop piano.

Tuning

As previously stated, toy pianos are playfully "out of tune" with a music box like quality, because they use metal tines to produce sound. Though most toy pianists embrace the whimsical qualities of toy piano tunings, some players choose to alter their instruments to fit closer to concert pitch. Other players may choose to make adjustments to promote better overall resonance of the instrument in the case of damage or defect with a tine. Altering the pitch of singular bars can be achieved through filing the tine or wrapping a thin piece of metal wiring on the end of a tine. It is not recommended that beginner students attempt to tune their toy piano as once solid metal is altered it can never be restored and the toy piano will need to be replaced if a mistake is made in the alteration process. For those concerned about keeping their instruments, as close to factory tuning as possible it is paramount to avoid frequent tipping or upside-down storage of the instrument, as such placement or movement of the instrument will cause fluctuation in the tuning of the instrument. Likewise, as the tines are made of metal, rapid extreme climate changes will have an effect on the tuning of the instrument.

Toy piano maintenance

On the whole, toy pianos are generally very hardy instruments because their construction and design have been targeted to children, who are not always so kind to their toys. However, a common issue that may pop-up in transport or tipping of the instrument is that the plastic keys become a bit weebly-wobly. This can easily be fixed by gently running a hand across the keyboard.

WEEBLY-WOBLY KEYS

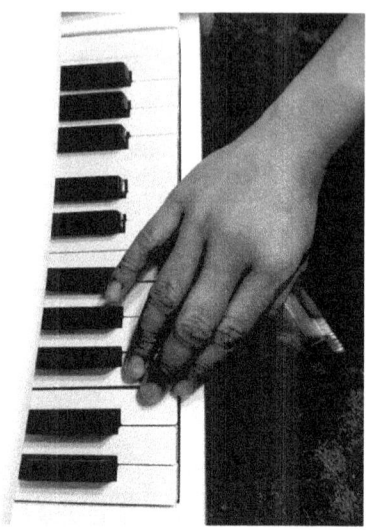
HAND RUNNING ACROSS THE KEYBOARD

Grand toy piano legs should be securely fastened and tightened as described in the assembly instructions included with your toy piano purchase. This allows the instrument to fully resonate and project sound effectively.

CHAPTER TWO
COMPOSERS & WRITING FOR TOY PIANO

The best composers and innovators of the musical language are ones who are always questioning and seeking new ways to express their inner feelings and artistic interpretations of extra-musical topics, from philosophy to nature to technology to the mystic and everything in between. Composers who gravitate to the toy piano have very different reasons and inspiration for using what was once considered a mere child's toy. Composing for toy piano requires a great deal of imagination and an understanding of the instruments quirks. Very few composers are successful at writing works for toy piano with no prior knowledge or physical experience with the instrument. Even with the varied rages of toy piano models, a composer is faced with three octaves or less in range and must carefully consider where they will place their melodies and harmonies. Due to the primitive nature of the keyboard mechanism compared to the complexity of a traditional piano, and the individuality of each toy piano; repeated notes can sometimes be problematic, as a key may not return as quickly as the composer anticipates. The shortened size of the keys can create anatomical difficulty for some adults in continual fast sweeping or long tremolo sections over a wide hand span due to playing position limitations, in addition to, a small lip of wood from the top of the instrument that subtly extends just over the keys of many toy pianos. Concert grand pianos are on the whole, more reliable instruments but are a few hundred dollars more expensive than their entry-level tabletop counterparts. Other peculiarities for the composer to consider include: possible anatomical limitations from modifications to the standard playing position, the inability to sustain notes longer than the natural decay time once a tine is struck (a quality that varies from toy piano to toy piano), the dynamic range of the instrument, the limited ability to project over large or particularly loud ensembles, the fact that it does not tune to concert pitch, and that it has a natural percussive key noise sound which also varies from instrument to instrument and model to model. Composers interested in writing for toy piano should make the investment to purchase or borrow an instrument from a colleague, because the toy piano must be tangibly experienced to truly exploit its strengths and understand its weaknesses.

As mentioned in the preface, there is a revival of the toy piano as a concert instrument and with that are a number of new works that are being created for solo toy piano as well as the implementation of toy piano in chamber ensembles, **electroacoustic** works, as well as works employing the use of **live electronics** and **found objects**. While composing for toy piano can present a number of unusual challenges, it can also be a very rewarding experience. There's nothing quite like a toy piano performance and due to the individuality of toy pianos, no performance of a toy piano piece is exactly the same.

The following highlights of composers, who have written for toy piano is by no means exhaustive or completely focused on each composers' use of toy piano in their works. Notable works for listening are highlighted for each composer, and where possible for living composers a link to their professional website has been included for further listening.

John Cage
Full Name: John Milton Cage, Jr.
Dates: September 5, 1912 – August 12, 1992
Country: United States of America
Notable Works: *4'33', Suite for Toy Piano, A Valentine Out of Season, Music for Marcel Duchamp, Sonatas and Interludes*

John Cage is perhaps best known by the outside world as the composer of "the silent piece." Musicians and new music junkies refer to the work by it's actual name *4'33"*. The work was a shock when it was premiered by the accomplished new music pianist David Tudor; sitting in silence at a closed piano with a stopwatch for exactly four minutes and thirty-three seconds. On the surface, this piece seems absurd, but John Cage's music is often about a concept or deeper meaning; he is looking to impart upon his audience as well as an inner philosophical discourse. If an audience member, takes the time to really experience 4'33", they will notice something very profound... There is no such thing as silence! The hum of the air conditioning, the cough of the elderly gentleman in the back of the hall, the squeak of a chair, the unwrapping of candy, the street noise from cars passing outside, the sounds of our organic functions even follow us into an anechoic chamber... the sensation of our blood pumping, our breath... all of these sounds are embedded into the fabric of our existence and in 4'33" we are faced with this glaring reality.

From 1933 to 1957, an institution called Black Mountain College in Asheville, North Carolina was the stage for a motley crew of liberal arts faculty that would push the boundaries of then accepted norms in education and presentation of various media from the visual to dance to music and beyond. John Cage and his partner Merce Cunningham were faculty members at Black Mountain College and it was here that Cage penned the iconic **Suite for Toy Piano (1948)**. If you look at a score of the suite, the first thing one notices is that while the work lies comfortably in the range of toy piano, it is actually scored for the traditional piano. Some movements use the grand staff, while others have only one staff and use either treble or bass clef. Such a scoring decision means the piece can be played on a traditional 88-key piano as well as toy piano. A practical reason for this notation decision may be that many of Cage's works, from the time he met Merce Cunningham, were made for cutting edge presentations of dance and music in non-traditional venues that Cunningham and Cage referred to as **happenings**. A set of interesting facts to give the reader an idea of the process include: Cunningham's dancers were trained in silence; Cunningham's works were choreographed to stopwatch timings; Cunningham and Cage often created the music and the dance separately only joining them for dress rehearsal or the final performance. Cage also, held firm to the belief that a work was not completed until he was able to secure a performance of the work, and this could have also had influence on his scoring choices in the *Suite for Toy Piano*.

Suite for Toy Piano easily became a standard in the repertoire of anyone seeking to seriously study toy piano as a professional musician because it does not use electronics (which are often daunting to many classically trained pianists), and access to the score is easy thanks to Cage's contract with Peters Publishing, which has worldwide distribution.

George Crumb
Full Name: George Crumb
Dates: October 24, 1929 - Present
Country: United States of America
Notable Works: *Ancient Voices of Children, Black Angels, Vox Balaenae, and A Little Suite for Christmas, A.D. 1979*

The first image that comes to mind for any musician that has played from a Crumb score is perhaps the odd paper size of the sheet music; Crumb initially chose to make his music on over-sized paper, so that it was difficult to copy his scores on a standard photocopier, which decreased copyright infringement of Crumb's music. The next quality of Crumb's works that strikes the ear is his mastery of **extended techniques** for both voice as well as instruments. These extended techniques include gestures such as using a mallet on an upright bass, or playing the strings on the inside of a traditional piano. Though Crumb does not compose for electronics, he does use amplification of acoustic instruments for a number of his compositions.

Crumb holds an impressive set of honorary degrees and awards, most notably he won the Pulitzer Prize in 1968 for his work *Echoes of Time and the River*, and Grammy Award for Best Contemporary Composition in 2000 for the composition *Star-Child*.

George Crumb served for over thirty years as a professor at the University of Pennsylvania before he retired to his home in Pennsylvania where he continues to compose and supervises the recoding of his entire catalogue of works to be released by Bridge Records.

His most notable work employing the use of toy piano is *Ancient Voices of Children*.

Mauricio Kagel
Full Name: Mauricio Kagel
Dates: December 24, 1931 – September 18, 2008
Country: Argentina
Notable Works: *String Sextet, Rrrrrr, Musik für Renaissance-Instrumente, Les idées fixes,*

Mauricio Kagel was born in Buenos Aires in 1931 to a Jewish family of both Russian and German ancestry. As a child, Kagel took voice, conducting, piano, cello, and organ lessons. One of his early teachers included legendary Argentine composer Alberto Ginastera. Kagel spent a considerable amount of time studying philosophy and literature, which shaped a lot of his thoughts on music, as evidenced by his preoccupation with writing works that are based on themes of paradox and irony. In 1950, at the age of 19, his first composition was published and seven years later he moved to Cologne in Germany on a scholarship, where he maintained a home base for the rest of his life. In 1969, twenty years after his first composition was published, Kagel was appointed director of the Institute of New Music at the Rheinische Musikschule in Cologne.

Kagel, was very aware that for many listeners encountering new music today, completely improvised, structured improvisation, and strictly notated music, sound incredibly similar. Yet, he continually sought to create a body of work that had great variation; to that end, he worked outside the traditional parameters of music composition, beyond his use of unusual instruments and extended techniques for conventional instruments, Kagel was active in film, radio plays, stage works, and other visual media. He maintained a journal with thoughts for new pieces, many of which were conceptual or theatrical in nature.

Julia Wolfe
Full Name: Julia Wolfe
Dates: December 18, 1958 – Present
Country: United States of America
Notable Works: *East Broadway (1996), My Beautiful Scream (2003), Anthracite Fields* (2014) *2015 Pulitzer Prize Winner*
Website: juliawolfemusic.com

In 2015, Julia Wolfe was awarded the coveted Pulitzer Prize in music for her work *Anthracite Fields (2014)*, but her vast catalogue features works for all manner of ensembles and soloists. Wolfe's impressive body of work blends the academic music tradition with rock, folk music, and pop culture, often resulting in works that feature non-traditional ensemble members such as a DJ and electric guitar, alongside conventional performers such as baroque strings, classically trained vocalists, and others.

East Broadway composed in 1996 for toy piano and playback, has become, much like Cage's *Suite for Toy Piano*, a staple of the concert repertoire, and performances of the work can easily be found by a number of toy pianists worldwide on the Internet in video and audio recording formats. Ironically, *East Broadway* is the only piece Wolfe has composed and released for toy piano solo. The captivating three-minute work was commissioned by toy piano virtuoso Margret Leng Tan and then premiered by Tan in France in 1997.

Karlheinz Essl
Full Name: Karlheinz Essl, Jr.
Dates: August 15, 1960 - Present
Country: Austria
Notable Works: *Kalimba (2005), Sequitur V (2008), WebernSpielWerk (2005), Listen Thing (2008), Whatever shall be (2010), under wood (2012), Miles to go (2012), Pachinko (2014), VIRIBVS VNITIS (2014)*
Website: essl.at

Dr. Karlheinz Essl, Jr. is an Austrian composer who has studied as well as taught in some of the most illustrious music conservatories and programs throughout Europe. Dr. Essl's first auditory interaction was not a positive one, he speaks of writing the instrument off, toy pianist Isabel Ettenauer loaned him a toy piano and he began to experiment with the sound possibilities. In 2013, Dr. Essl released, **whatever shall be**, an album featuring most of his toy piano works performed by Isabel Ettenauer, this CD and other recordings of his toy piano pieces can be located on his website **essl.at**.

In composing for the toy piano he believes that one must spend significant time with the instrument because, while it looks similar to the traditional piano it is a completely different instrument and must be considered for the purpose of composition in a special manner. His compositions for toy piano, Dr. Essl have largely sought to embrace a fresh aspect of the toy piano for each work; whether employing electronics or partnering the toy piano with another instrument or ensemble, Essl feels that the toy piano is most palatable for the audience when it is in conversation with another sound source. Dr. Essl does not look to repeat a particular sound or aesthetic of a work using toy piano more than once, which is why each one of his works for toy piano possesses a different sound and employs a different method of interaction with the toy piano.

Tristan Perich
Full Name: Tristan Perich
Dates: 1982 to Present
Country: United States of America
Notable Works: *qsqsqsqsqqqqqqqqqq, Surface Image,*
Website: www.tristanperich.com

Tristan Perich is a New York based sound artist and composer, working within the electronic medium. Perich specializes in the use of 1-bit sound, which he marries with acoustic instruments. Perich is a master of sound installations and his impressive body of work, has been presented, multiple times throughout the world. *Qsqsqsqsqqqqqqqqqq*, Perich's work for three toy pianos and 1-bit symphony, has been performed on over 47 occasions worldwide and to date is his only work for toy piano.

CHAPTER THREE
NOTABLE PLAYERS

Margret Leng Tan

"I was so pushing the envelope of the piano, taking it to its ultimate boundaries, its ultimate frontiers, that I fell off the edge and landed on the toy piano." - Margret Leng Tan in Sorceress of the New Piano (2004)

Margret Leng Tan has a long decorated career as a toy pianist and interpreter of new music, though she did not begin life as a toy pianist, and after becoming the first woman to earn a doctorate from The Juilliard School Tan briefly took a break from life as a professional musician to pursue a career training hearing-assist dogs. Tan was born in Singapore in 1945, and began her musical career at a very early age, first spending hours practicing on violin before moving to full-sized pianos. At age 16 she left Singapore on her own to begin her studies at Juilliard. Tan states that she is incredibly obsessive by nature, a quality that has been at times paralyzing, but that she has learned to use for her benefit as an unseen motivator to push herself as well as her art to new heights of accomplishment.

Following her short stint as a dog trainer, Tan set out to explore the intersections of Asian and Western music. The quest invariably led her to the work of John Cage, who frequently incorporated Eastern methodology and culture (notably his use of the I-Ching in composition, paired with his penchant for Eastern musical instruments, and his Western musical training). Tan met Cage in the 1980s and began collaborating with him until his death in 1992. Tan quickly became the most celebrated interpreter of Cage's works for keyboard instruments. Ironically Tan, did not purchase a toy piano until 1993, when she was scheduled to perform Cage's *Suite for Toy Piano* at The Lincoln Center in New York, the year after Cage's death. That first toy piano came from a humble New York City thrift store and by 1997 Tan had released a complete album of toy piano works *The Art of the Toy Piano*, which firmly solidified her place as the world's first toy piano virtuoso and created a strong case for the toy piano as a serious concert instrument.

Tan is a champion of both the toy piano and new music, which has led to numerous works being composed for her to premiere and promote by the world's top composers including, Tan Dun (China), Julia Wolfe (USA), Michael Nyman (United Kingdom), and legendary American composer George Crumb. Today, Margret Leng Tan maintains an active career as both a pianist and toy pianist, performing at festivals across the globe, in addition to recordings of avant-garde works for new albums and television.

www.margaretlengtan.com

Phyllis Chen

New York City based composer and performer Phyllis Chen first encountered the toy piano at a puppet theater in Chicago in her early-twenties, and gave her first public performance on toy piano in 2001 in Chicago, but it wasn't initially her first priority as a professional artist. During her doctoral studies at Indiana University, Chen developed tendonitis, an injury that has been known to prematurely end or significantly alter the trajectory of many musicians' careers. For Chen, it took almost two years to recover, during which time she began to ruminate on her artistic goals. Because toy pianos are less stressful on the anatomy, than a traditional piano, Chen was able to practice on toy pianos during her convalescence, and maintain a connection to music during a challenging time. Chen has spoken in interviews of the freedom that comes from the fact that the toy piano does not have the same regimented history of repertoire that the traditional piano maintains. In 2007 she founded the UnCaged Toy Piano Festival in New York City, which exists to expand interest and build new repertoire for the toy piano. The UnCaged Toy Piano Festival draws in participants and audience members from across the globe, toy piano virtuoso Margret Leng Tan has been a performer on more than one occasion. UnCaged concerts take place across New York City in a variety of venue types and there is an open call for compositions every year. Chen is also, an active member of the International Contemporary Ensemble and continues to receive praise for her work on the traditional full-size piano as well as on her collection of toy pianos.

Chen sees the toy piano as a unique opportunity for a pianist to be a multi-instrumentalist, since most new works for toy piano incorporate other instruments, whether conventional or otherwise. In her own compositions, Chen uses kitchen mixing bowls, gongs, music boxes, and found objects. Chen also, has a passion for uniting toy piano performance with visual elements and to that end she has collaborated on numerous occasions with digital media artist Rob Dietz, producing miniature theatrical works. Her work, has garnered international attention, resulting in numerous commissions from ensembles and organizations from the Baryshnikov Center to ICElab Series to the Singapore International Festival of the Arts, along with grants from New Music USA and the Foundation for the Contemporary Arts.

www.phyllischen.net

Isabel Ettenauer

Austrian toy pianist Isabel Ettenauer started her musical life on an orange 20-key Bontempi toy piano at age four but moved up to a concert grand piano when she began taking traditional piano lessons. Like many toy pianists, her passion for toy piano came when she began to study the music of John Cage but she was also aware that many other composers after Cage had and were continuing to experiment with writing for toy piano. Ettenauer was already familiar with the works of American composer Stephen Montague and knew of his work *Mirabella* for three-octave toy piano. Eventually, Ettenauer invested in the importation of some toy pianos from America, and after their arrival in 1999 she very rapidly made the decision to begin commissioning works for toy piano. To date, various composers, including Karlheinz Essl, have composed over thirty works for Ettenauer.

www.isabelettenauer.com

Xenia Pestova

Russian pianist Xenia Pestova has a penchant for exploration of keyboard instruments. Pestova has been commissioned pieces for the toy piano, collaborated with inventors of the ROLI Seaboard (a new soft continuous keyboard, which offers the player control over the attack, sustain, and decay of tones), and inspired composers to create new pieces for the Indian Harmonium. She was a featured performer at the World Toy Piano Summit at Festival Rainy Days in Luxembourg. Pestova has studied at music institutions and programs across the globe, from New Zealand to the United Kingdom to France to the Netherlands to Canada. She is currently the Director of Performance at the University of Nottingham in the United Kingdom.

www.xeniapestova.com

CHAPTER FOUR
MODERN PRODUCTION TOY PIANO MODELS

While there are many oddities in the toy piano world still left from the experimentation days before the industry became largely standardized by the addition of modern mechanical equipment to the production process, most modern toy pianos come in three flavors: tabletop, spinet or upright, and grand.

Tabletop models

Generally consisting of 18-25 keys, tabletop models are intended for use on a table and do not come with benches. These models may also be comfortably played whilst sitting on the floor with legs crossed. These pianos are the most portable and can easily be stored in a cupboard or other out-of-the-way storage solution when not in use.

Upright and spinet models

Ranging from 25-37 keys, these larger models look like their traditional upright and spinet 88-key cousins. They easily fit against a wall and take up minimal space. They frequently come with a matching bench, made in proportion with the size of the piano.

Grand models

Grand toy pianos come in a number of flavors and sizes from 30-key to full 37-key concert grand models with opening lids. These pianos look just like their larger concert grand piano cousins. The concert grand model is the most common for Schoenhut artists and professional musicians. While the matching benches for these models were originally developed for children, they comfortably hold the weight of an average adult without falling apart. Tabletop grand toy piano models also exist, and possess incredibly short legs as well as smaller ranges than full sized 37-key concert grand toy pianos.

CHAPTER FIVE
PRINCIPLES OF TECHNIQUE

A habit, once formed, is difficult to break, and frequently becomes an obstacle to successful development on an instrument. This is why it is so important to pay significant attention to consistent use of proper technique in the early days of learning an instrument. Bad habits can also, lead to injuries that effectively end one's journey on an instrument; whether that is a journey of enjoyment as a hobby or a journey to become a professional musician, it is a heartbreaking conclusion. There are many schools of thought when it comes to playing technique that stem from cultural tradition among other sources, but the average healthy individual without impairment to basic range of motion should be able to play the piano and toy piano without physical pain. This text has been developed along with companion exercises in the back of the book, alongside, a continually updated Soundcloud profile and YouTube channel that breaks down many of these playing techniques for visual as well as aural orientated learners.

Playing positions
Tabletop models
Tabletop pianos, as one can surmise from the name were designed for use on a table, but they are just as easy to use while seated on the floor. Professional artists, performing pieces for two toy pianos often choose to use a tabletop model in tandem with a concert grand model, placing the tabletop piano on a low stool or short box to keep the keyboard levels of each piano as close to each other as possible. Tabletop models are an excellent choice for beginning toy piano enthusiasts because they are quite affordable, portable, and easy to store. Furthermore, for adult students with mobility issues, tabletop pianos, which can be played from a regular chair, offer a level of comfort that the matching low bench of a concert grand does not offer. The only tricky part of using a tabletop piano comes in trying to find the right table or elevated surface to practice. It is paramount to cultivating a relaxed and injury free playing technique that one locates a practice surface that is not too high or too low. Surfaces that are too high can result in shoulder fatigue that decreases the time one is able to comfortably practice, while surfaces that are too low can result in back pain from the inevitable "hunched" position one must take to reach the keys. The optimal practice surface is one where the player's arms, shoulders, and back are in the most relaxed placement for their individual autonomy. Every body is different and will necessitate a different table size if they choose to play on a raised surface. In contrast, the issues of finding the correct chair or raised surface are of rare concern, if one is sitting on the floor to play the toy piano.

Playing Position Examples for Tabletop Models

PIANO ON A RAISED SURFACE

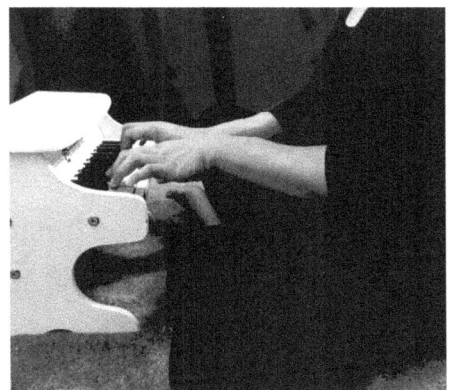

PIANO ON FLOOR

Grand, upright, and spinet models

As previously stated, concert grand models with an opening top are the preferred models for professional toy piano artists. Some artists choose not to put the legs on the toy piano, opting to treat the instrument as a larger tabletop model; however, doing so decreases the resonance and projection of the instrument even if the top is open. While there isn't a standard for an adult sitting at a grand toy piano, a couple of options are demonstrated in the following photos. Special circumstances and extended playing techniques (such as foot pedals or electronic processing) may necessitate a change in sitting position for grand toy pianos. The playing position for upright and spinet models is similar to that of grand toy pianos; however, due to their design one cannot put their legs underneath upright or spinet models. There are photographed instances of players using regular chairs to play upright models, which can be achieved by raising the level of the instrument to be in proportion with the height of the standard chair, often by placing the upright model on a wooden platform. Elevating the toy piano on a wooden platform has the additional effect of enhancing the projection of the instrument.

Playing Position Examples for Grand Toy Piano Models

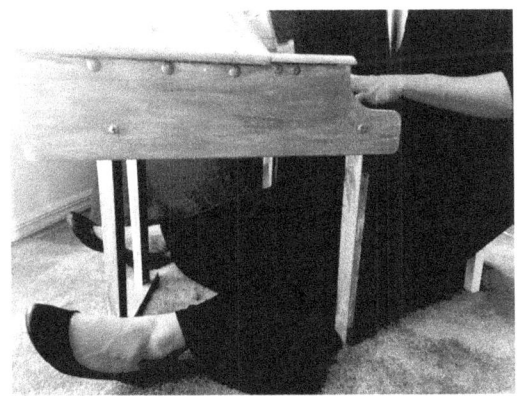

LEGS UNDER

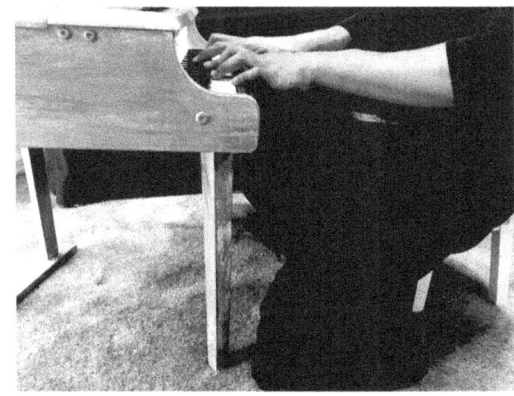

CROSSED LEGS

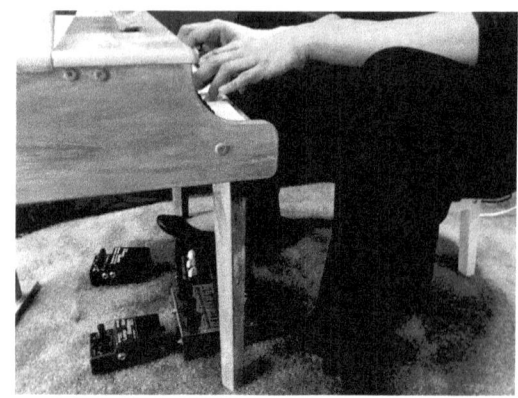

KNEES UP, USED FOR EXTENDED TECHNIQUES BECAUSE THIS POSITION LIMITS THE RANGE OF MOTION OF THE ARMS.

Range of motion

Just because the toy piano requires less physical weight to depress a key, does not mean that one should neglect the proper and healthy technique one uses to play a large 88-key traditional piano. Understanding the anatomical range of motion of the major body parts involved in piano playing is crucial to developing and maintaining proper technique, which at the end of the day leads to strong expression of music and injury prevention. Advanced piano playing requires a sensitive understanding and control of muscle groups, boney structures, and sinuous anatomy spanning from head to toe. A common misconception is that piano playing comes from the fingers, because the fingers visibly engage with the keyboard; but muscles directly connected to the fingers are small, weak, and easily prone to injury. Further, playing from the fingers does not require the performer to physically engage with the music in a manner, which puts the rhythm of the music (no matter how seemingly complex or disjointed) into the artist's body. Feeling the arc of a phrase, the ebb and flow of the total structure is paramount to presenting an artistic performance of a work.

The creation of music is a nuanced dance between the mind and the body, which takes internalized musical phrases and translates them to the physical act of piano playing an instrument. There tends to be a lot of mystery and erroneous terminology surrounding the act of playing; many people try to liken certain aspects of playing to other instruments and their sound production. The fact of the matter is that the piano and toy piano produce sound by means of a hammer striking an element (strings/tine) causing vibration. There is an initial attack, the sound sustains and dies away at a natural rate for the instrument and performance space; barring extended techniques and the use of electronics, traditional acoustic sound production is limited to the natural attack, sustain, and decay process. Other limitations that must be accepted are those of the player's body. The human body while an incredibly remarkable system is limited in mobility. One has bones, hard structures that will only move so far and surrounding these bones are muscle groups, which are also limited how far they can move in relation to each other as well as their relation to the skeletal structure to which they are invariably tied. Once these concepts are accepted in the student's mind, they can begin to fully embrace the strengths of the body, and interact with the keyboard mechanism in a purposeful manner.

Torso

The first place one should feel the phrase, fundamental rhythm, and the overall arc of a composition is from the torso. It rotates around the body's center of gravity, and this is initially, a great and important place to begin to feel music. The torso must feel the continuous pulse of the music often referenced in this text as **fundamental rhythm**, it is not the pulse of the meter written on the page or signaled by a metronome marking, but rather it is the connected energy of the work that starts from the beginning of the piece, pushes forward, and hangs in the air just after the last note is sounded. Before, one strikes the first note of the work they must feel the fundamental rhythm radiating from the core of their being, otherwise their performance is nothing more than a robotic, computer generated, realization of the score in front of them. It is this connection with fundamental rhythm and the ability to shape the rolling energy from the first note to the last that sets professional performers apart from hobbyists. The connection with fundamental rhythm, which starts in the torso, is something that one must always be aware of particularly, in the beginning of studies when one is encountered with the massive list of things that the mind and body must coordinate to produce a cohesive interpretation of the notes on the page.

Arms

Energy and transfer of the fundamental rhythm moves from the torso, which essentially acts as a fulcrum, to the arm. On a large piano, the arm must additionally compensate for space across a long expanse; on the toy piano, the keyboard spatial plane is more compact, but that doesn't mean that the flow of energy from the core to the arm can afford to be lost, because it is this critical energy that must pass through the arm to the wrist and finally engage the fingers.

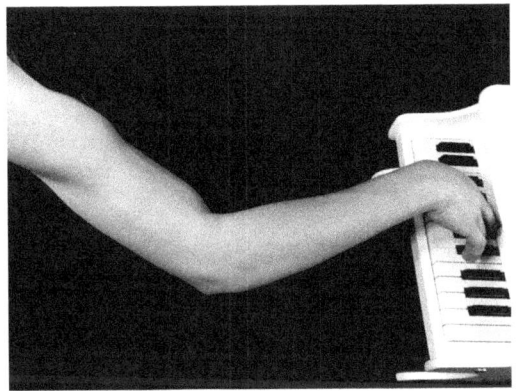 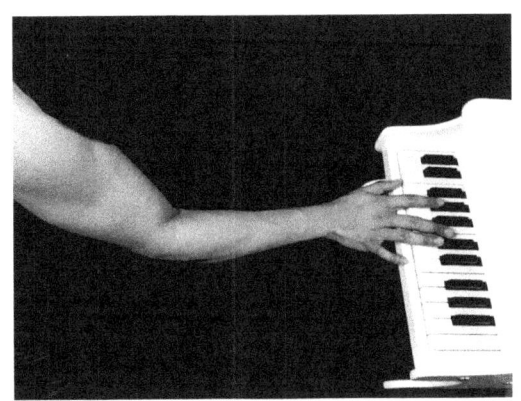

Wrist

The wrist is the most mobile of the joints involved in playing the piano, though it too has limitations in range of motion. The flow of energy follows a cycle from the initial conceptualization of fundamental rhythm in the mind to the torso to the forearm to the elbow and now to the hand via the wrist action. The wrist has the largest range of motion up and down and though adept at left, and right movement; the span of the wrist movement from side to side is smaller than that of up and down. The pianist must use this spatial gift to their advantage. As the plane the keyboard does not change, it is easy to become stuck in a single spatial position leading to music made chiefly from the fingers. When playing comes from the fingers alone, musicality suffers; a break in fundamental rhythm, and memory slips are the first side-effects of finger-centric technique; however, it is the later side effects that are the most crippling... literally. Finger-centric playing can result in injuries from repetitive motion syndrome, to carpal tunnel, and other career ending injuries. Even a hobby player could end a promising journey to proficiency from improper technique. The practitioner who understands that even a single note can be attacked from various places above and below the center plane of play; who uses the method of sending energy from the torso and employing all the muscles and joints to their advantage, can avoid common injuries and have a truly joyful experience with the instrument. At no point should piano playing hurt... if it does one should immediately do a tension check at the first sight of pain, reevaluate their playing position, and following a break begin to practice again SLOWLY checking over their technique for repetitive action and tension. If the problem persists one should visit a qualified piano teacher, medical professional, and Alexander Technique specialist.

Range of Motion of the Wrist

CENTER

LEFT

RIGHT

MIDDLE

UP

DOWN

Fingers

The fingers are the last in the energy chain to the keyboard. This means, in some cases, that for advanced players, the beginner or traditional fingerings may be cast aside for ones that possess personal anatomical ease. In this book, specific fingerings may be given to introduce traditional fingering preferences; advanced players, may choose to substitute these suggestions for their own. In traditional sheet music publishing, editors place fingerings in scholarly versions of scores known as urtext editions, these should be interpreted as general suggestions, rather than firm law. While it is paramount to have a relaxed and natural hand position at the keys, too many method books and piano instructors get so caught up in obsessing over fingerings and hand position playing that the student never develops an understanding of fundamental rhythm. The byproduct of this oversight is in the student's education is clunky playing, which lacks a musical soul. For students, hoping to move from a toy piano to a traditional piano, the obsession with finger and position based playing does nothing to help them navigate the wide expanse of an 88-key piano. The student should not only internally hear the next tone in the sequence of the piece before it is played but they should have a reliable intuition of where that pitch exists along the span of the keyboard.

Finger or position playing does not and cannot develop this necessary spatial understanding. The toy piano with it's compact range, in proportion to the average child, teaches this awareness so that when the child graduates to the larger 88-key piano, the expanse seems less daunting. For adults, this understanding of the spatial relationship of where exactly a specific note lies on the toy piano feels different, as it takes less effort for an adult to cover the span of the keyboard, thus this awareness falls to fine motor skills; and less energy from the large muscle groups in the arm and torso is needed.

While fingers are the last to engage from an energy perspective, they are in many cases the first place to gather tension. Fingers can only extend and flex, but they are a primary fixation because our eyes fall upon them first. The beginning student should always check their fingers for tension. Are you locking your joints? Does it hurt when you play? Is it difficult to move from one gesture to another because your fingers feel stiff? These are questions one should as they practice. Additionally, it is recommended that one obtains a cheap floor length mirror or uses a video recording device such as a cell phone to monitor progress, in addition to critiquing tension and other technical mistakes. A complete section addressing healthy practice methods is located later in this text.

One hand or two hands?

In view of the small range of the toy piano and by virtue of the fact its keys are relatively small, an adult can comfortably play the instrument with one hand. Two hands become necessary when the range of a composition extends beyond the player's hand span or when several voices (melodic lines) are being played simultaneously. Another reason a performer might use two hands is to play works composed for one pianist and two toy pianos, which is a common occurrence in the toy piano literature; as the instruments do not take up a great deal of space they can easily be arranged in front of a performer for simultaneous play.

ONE HAND

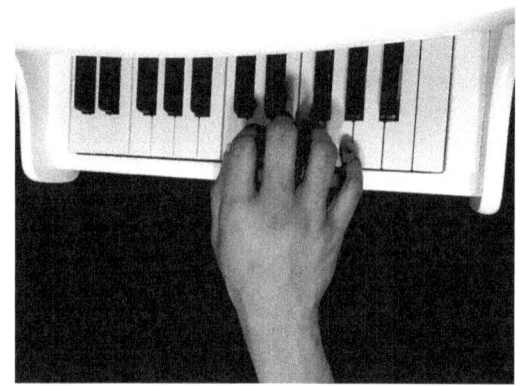 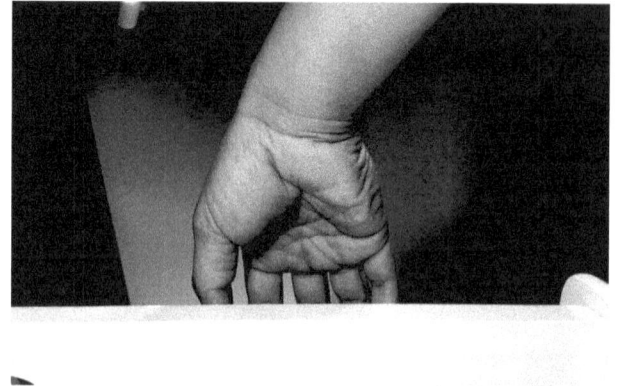

ABOVE **BELOW**

TWO HANDS

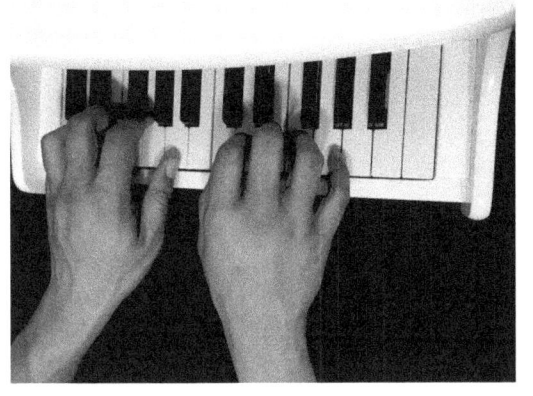 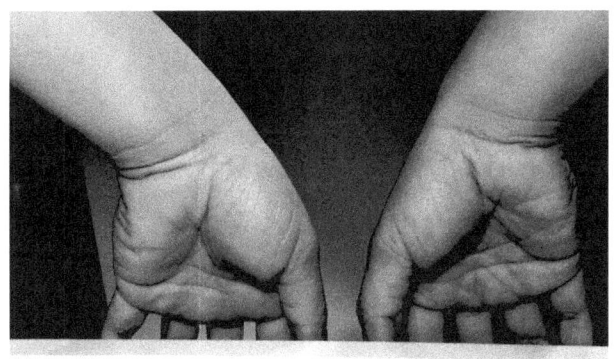

ABOVE **BELOW**

Companion resources for this text...

YouTube channel: Toyager Toy Piano Method

Soundcloud: soundcloud.com/toyager

To purchase your own toy piano...

Schoenhut Piano Company Inc.

6480-B US 1 North
St. Augustine, FL 32095

Website: toypiano.com

Email: info@toypiano.com

Phone: (904) 810-1945

Office Hours: Monday – Friday // 8:00 AM - 4:30 PM EST

UNDERSTANDING MUSIC NOTATION

CHAPTER SIX
COMMON QUESTIONS

Is notation necessary to play music?

A very common argument, in the modern world of technology, where most things are learned from watching YouTube videos, is that music notation is obsolete and otherwise unnecessary to the process of learning to play an instrument. The problem with YouTube is that anybody can put up a video, without proper training or technique and then spread their bad habits to a sea of followers by exploiting a popular tune, trendy artist, or working another kitschy angle. Beyond the promotion of poor technique, learning how to read and interpret musical notation is important for those wanting to extend beyond the realm of hobbyist into professional or semi-professional musician, whether as a performer or composer. To take the concept out of the musical realm, imagine you are planning a trip to Spain, you have at least a year before you leave, and you do not speak Spanish. Sure, you could easily experience the tourist attractions and have a wonderful vacation, but imagine the time you would have if you spoke even simple conversational Spanish; with your understanding of the language you are able to travel off the beaten path, to communicate with the locals, read newspapers to get a feel for how the locals think. In the end, your study of the language enhances your absorption of the culture of Spain. The same principle applies to the study of musical language.

Why was notation developed?

The earliest music was largely improvised, or rather made up in real time. Even at the dawn of the 16th century when notated music started to hit its stride, performing musicians were expected to be able to improvise. Musicians specializing in keyboard instruments such as the harpsichord, clavichord, organ, and others were expected to be able to improvise at sight based on a system of notation called **figured bass**. (Numbers underneath the lowest member of a staff system, which typically employed the bass clef, and outlined basic harmonies for the keyboardist, are known as figured bass.) Notation was developed from the need and compulsion to replay pieces that people loved. In a time long before commercial recording and personal playback devices, a system had to be created which was specific and yet simple enough to be decoded by musicians across the Western musical world, regardless of native language.

When was standard notation created?

Experimentation with notation systems has been in existence since man carved into rock, scholars have been trying to decode Greek music notation for centuries, Renaissance monks spent hours creating ornate hymn books with ornate illuminated manuscript, and composers today constantly push the bounds of what is "the norm" for music notation. The Western standard notation we use today began in the 11th century when specific pitches were assigned to points in space on a system of lines and spaces. Notation language evolved through the next several centuries, creating more detail for faster rhythms, articulations, and other changes until the early 17th century when almost all traces of earlier systems had been phased out. With a notation system that was largely standardized across Europe, composers could focus on writing some of the most complex and cutting edge music of their day. These musical pioneers would push boundaries so far that a standardized tuning system would emerge to supply the demand of the tonally complex new music that was being composed.

Over 200 years after it found standardized footing in royal courts, churches, and the performance halls of the bourgeois, across Europe; musicians continue to use the same system of musical notation. While the fact that the same notation system has been in use for hundreds of years may make it seem boring or antiquated, such standardization affords us a unique link to our musical heritage. It is because of the relative stability of our Western musical notation system that opera companies worldwide can perform works by Verdi and Puccini, organists can command hair-raising performances of works by Bach, and brides can walk down the aisle to a march from incidental music for Shakespeare's *A Midsummer Night's Dream* as penned by the composer Felix Mendelssohn over 160 years ago.

Unconventional notation systems

Graphic notation

Around 1950, experimental and avant-garde composers began experimenting with new visual representations that exist outside of the standard notation system. Graphic notation invites open interpretations of works because each musician interprets the pictures and symbols differently. Graphic notation makes the performer an active collaborator alongside the composer in the realization of the composition. This is a stark contrast to the current trend in conventionally notated music where many young academics are overly insistent on performers realizing their scores as close to the computer playback of the work from the notation software prevalent in the contemporary composition process. Some graphic scores may completely implement visual elements while others intertwine standard notation with graphic notation.

Text notation

Text notation also appears in 20th century music as composers begin to stretch the boundaries of sonic possibilities through a combination of embracing new technologies in electronic music as well as accepting the ideas of music philosophers such as John Cage, who were beginning to classify all sounds, even the "sound of silence", as valid musical sounds. All of a sudden, a toaster is a musical instrument, and the most logical method of informing the performer of the sounds the composer wants to come from the toaster is with detailed text instructions.

Text notation, much like graphic notation, may incorporate a mix of notation styles, including timing which requires the player to listen for cues in **fixed media** (pre-recorded accompanying track) or must use a stopwatch/timer to execute specific gestures or sounds at a specific time in the score.

Structured improvisation

It is important to note that a free-ish form of music known as structured improvisation exists, which may or may not use notation whether standard or conventional to facilitate a performance. Structured improvisations run the gamut from improvised sections in jazz standards, to improvising ensembles with works that have a basic set of rules. The common thread among all structured improvisations, no matter how experimental and free form they may seem is that there are pre-planned or pre-agreed upon parameters in place.

CHAPTER SEVEN
COMMON NOTATION & SYMBOLS

Staff

The **staff** is a system of lines and spaces, which forms the foundation of Western notated music. The standard staff has five lines and four spaces. Non-pitched percussion may be noted on a single line. Guitar, bass, or lute parts are frequently notated in tablature, which is another system of lines in spaces, where each line corresponds to a string on the instrument. Rhythm exercises are often notated without lines and spaces but do use measure lines or bar lines.

Notes, which extend further above or below the standard staff are notated with the use of **ledger lines**. Special markings were also developed to compensate for notes that are several octaves below or above the standard staff system.

Bar lines

A **standard measure line** is a single light vertical line denoting the end or beginning of a measure. Many musicians simply refer to a standard measure line as a bar line, both terms are acceptable when speaking about music.

Light double bar lines denote the end of a section.

A light bar line followed by a dark bar line indicates the end of a piece

A double bar line featuring two dots around the center staff line is known as a **repeat sign**. A right repeat sign indicates that the performer is to repeat the section; either from the start of the piece or the closest forward or left repeat sign. In special circumstances, repeats may be indicated by text and other signs such as: **D.C. al Fine** (go back to the beginning and play until the bar marked Fine), **D.S. al Coda** (go back and play until the sign and jump to a **coda**, additional material at the end of a composition).

Musical Alphabet

The **musical alphabet** uses only the first seven letters of the English Alphabet (A, B, C, D, E, F, G) and repeats the cycle after A. The staff, in partnership with a symbol known as a clef, dictates where in the musical alphabet a particular letter, which correlates to a specific pitch, falls. There are many clefs, but the toy piano primarily concerns itself with the treble clef because the natural range of the toy piano extends above middle-C though most concert grand toy pianos extend a few notes below middle-C. While the range of the toy piano can be extended through the use of electronics, the preferred style of notation for players employs the treble clef.

Pitch Class refers to how high or low a note sounds. A0 is the lowest note on a full-sized piano, and the common reference note middle-C bears the pitch class of C3.

Treble Clef

The **treble clef** is also referred to as the **G-Clef** because the clef wraps around the line on the staff, which represents the pitch G above Middle-C. In the early days of music notation, clefs moved in order to keep as much of music on the staff to avoid excessive usage of **ledger lines**, additional lines added below or above the staff to extend the range beyond the standard staff. Today the G-Clef encircles the second line of the staff and does not move.

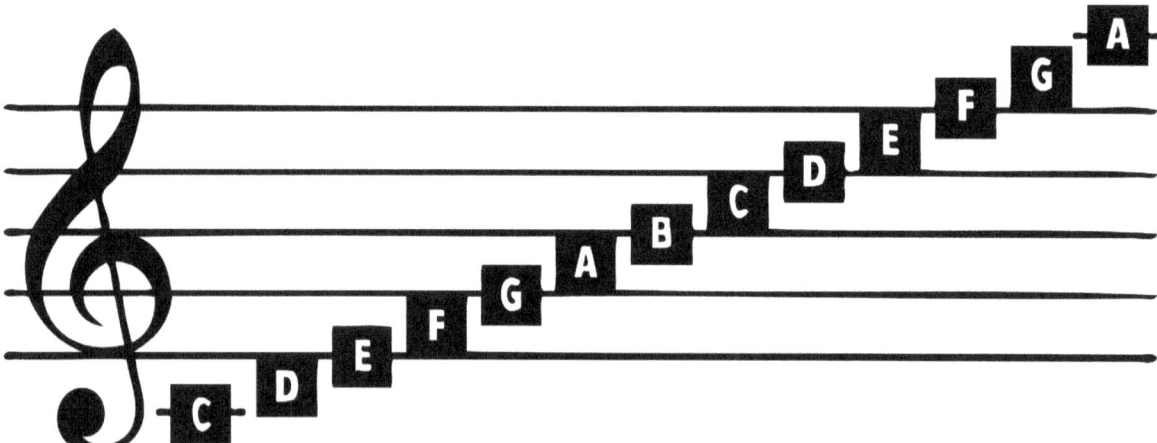

Notes & Rests

Whole Note	𝅝	4 beats	**Whole Rest**	𝄻	4 beats
Half Note	𝅗𝅥	2 beats	**Half Rest**	𝄼	2 beats
Quarter Note	♩	1 beat	**Quarter Rest**	𝄽	1 beat
Eighth Note	♪	½ beat	**Eighth Rest**	𝄾	½ beat
Sixteenth Note	𝅘𝅥𝅯	¼ beat	**Sixteenth Rest**	𝄿	¼ beat

The Dot

A dot following a note or rest indicates the addition of half the value of the note/rest before the dot.

For example, a half note with a dot works out this way:

> Half-note = 2 beats
>
> Dot = ½ of the value of a half-note = 1 beat
>
> 2 + 1 = 3
>
> Dotted half-note = 3 beats

Another great example, a whole-rest with a dot breaks down in the following manner:

> Whole-rest = 4 beats
>
> Dot = ½ of the value of a whole-rest = 2 beat
>
> 4 + 2 = 6
>
> Dotted whole-rest = 6 beats

Time Signature

Time signatures supply the player with two important pieces of information, and are expressed as a fraction.

Top number

How many beats are in a measure?

2 = 2 beats per measure

3 = 3 beats per measure

4 = 4 beats per measure

Bottom number

What type of note gets a beat?

1 = whole note

2 = half note

4 = quarter note

8 = eighth note

16 = sixteenth note

30

Tempo

Tempo is the rate at which a piece is played. Modern tempo markings may use specific metronome markings with either a note (such as a quarter note) = [insert number] or the abbreviation BPM (Beats Per Minute) = [insert number]. Earlier music pieces, frequently feature the Italian words, which we equate to modern BPM. In some scores the Italian tempo markings may be substituted for their French or German translations. These tempo markings in words also, have extra-musical implications, which are primarily concerned with the style of interpretation. Tempo can also be changed throughout a piece of music; a few common examples are included for study.

BPM Examples

♩ = 120   𝅗𝅥 = 60   ♪ = 144

Common Italian Markings

Grave	Very slow	25-45 BPM
Largo	Broadly	40-60 BPM
Adagio	Stately and with ease	66-70 BPM
Andante	At a walking pace	76-108 BPM
Moderato	Moderately	108-120 BPM
Allegro	Fast, bright	120-168 BPM
Vivace	Fast and lively	168-176 BPM
Presto	Very fast	168-200 BPM

Tempo alterations

Ritardando	Gradual slow in tempo	Abbreviation: *rit.*
Accelerando	Speeding up gradually	Abbreviation: *accel.*
a tempo	Back to the original tempo	
Rubato	Freedom to adjust the tempo for artistic interpretation	

Accidentals

Alterations to a **natural pitches** (the white keys on the standard keyboard), made by raising (sharp, #) or lowering by (flat, ♭) are called **accidentals**. While these alterations commonly pertain to the black keys on the keyboard but also translate to white keys in the case of these common **enharmonic equivalents**:

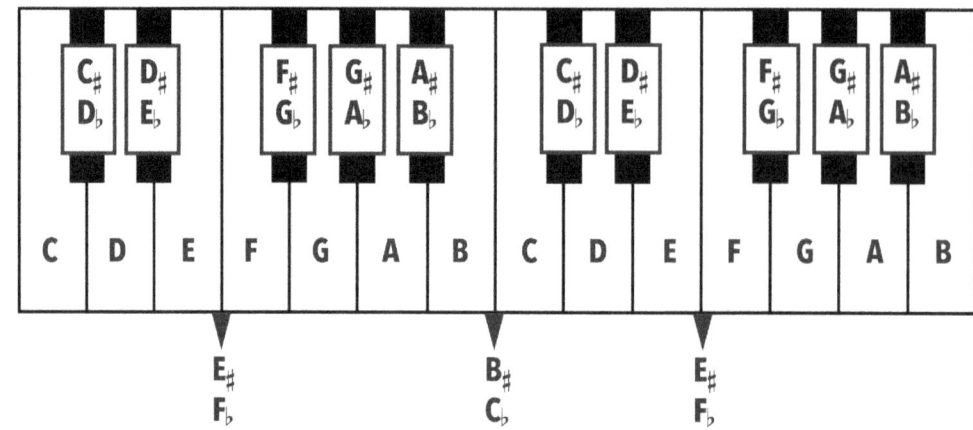

B# = C Natural

E# = F Natural

Enharmonic equivalents also apply to sharps and flats:
B-flat is the same as A-sharp and C-sharp is the same as D-flat.

When accidentals are notated on the staff, the accidental always goes to the left of the written note. In key signatures, accidentals at the beginning of the system are in effect unless a differing accidental symbol, directly in front of the note in question cancels the natural series of accidentals in the key signature. **Cautionary accidentals**, often in parentheses are there to remind the player of the accidentals native to the key signature, and occur after highly chromatic passages with accidentals outside the key signature. Another important rule to remember is that if an accidental is placed in front of a note and not part of a key signature, that accidental applies for the rest of the measure unless canceled by another accidental. ***For more examples and rules about accidentals on the staff, please review the written exercises in the back of the book.***

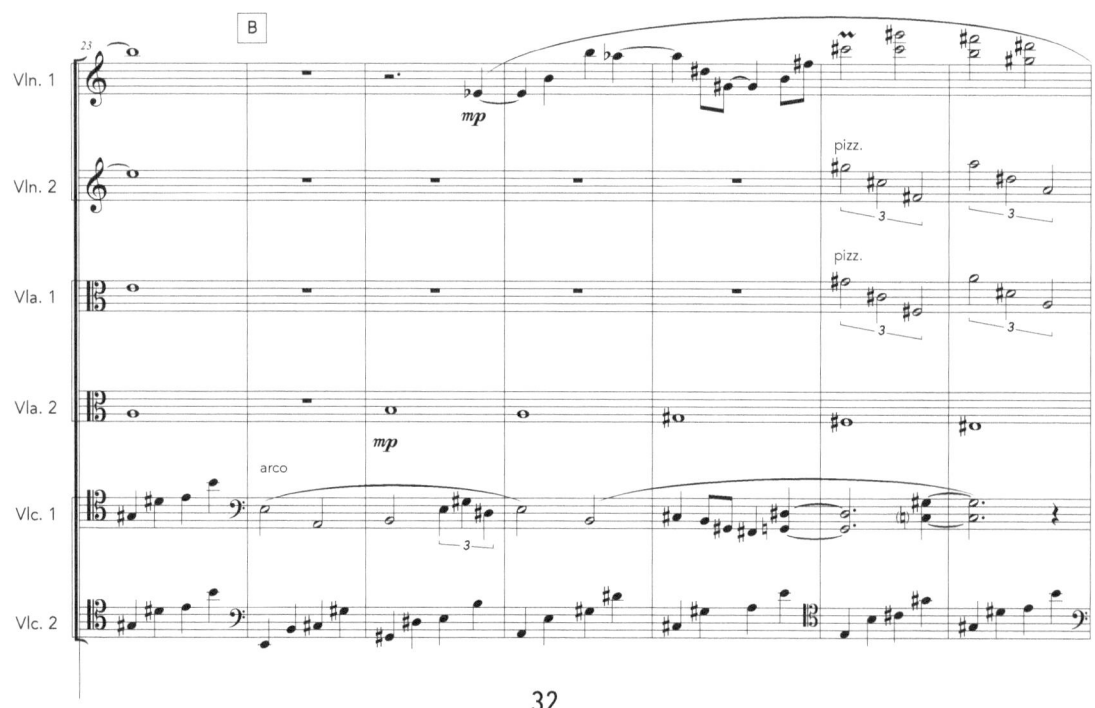

Dynamics

Dynamic markings are a key part of the Western musical notation system because they provide the performer with information about how loud or soft they are to play. Today composers may choose to write dynamic instructions for a performer in their native language, but the following Italian dynamic markings are still considered the standard:

Symbol	Long Form Name	Dynamic Value
pp	pianissimo	very soft
p	piano	soft
mp	mezzo piano	medium soft
mf	mezzo forte	medium loud
f	forte	loud
ff	fortissimo	very loud

As instruments evolved and became more powerful throughout the centuries, their dynamic capabilities improved as well; and so, notation of dynamic moved from "**terraced dynamics**" where things were suddenly soft or suddenly loud, to the widespread use of subtle and intense dynamic alterations with the most common markings being **crescendo** (getting louder) and **decrescendo** (getting softer). Because the playing mechanisms were designed to be durable and at the same time light enough for little hands to depress the keys, in general toy pianos have a small range of dynamics. A skilled toy pianist knows how to control the small dynamic range and can produce a masterful tone painting even with what some might consider a challenging range. Concert grand toy pianos have a deeper dynamic range because they have been designed for performance; however, from one concert grand to another there are variations in how loud or soft a performer can get before the sound of the keys becomes blaringly obvious. On a traditional large piano, one does not contend with as much key noise because the instrument has been nuanced for the reduction of such sounds. Composers looking to write for toy piano should take the natural "key noise" sound into account when writing for the instrument.

Articulation

Where dynamics address the subject of volume, articulation concerns the matter of the attack of notes. Both traditional piano and toy piano produce sound conventionally by means of a hammer striking strings or tines, which means that they have a fixed attack which cannot be altered. This fact means that many standard articulation markings are physically impossible for the acoustic keyboard instrument to execute; however, a rich heritage of their use in scores has fostered a tradition that continues today, no matter how erroneous in thought. Extended techniques allow the traditional string piano to transcend many of these limitations. For example, if one uses a series of fishing lines with rosin to "bow" the strings inside a piano many of the legato markings synonymous with writing for cello or viola are possible because sound is now being produced by a continuous source of friction exciting vibration versus the conventional hammer, which makes a single attack exciting the vibrating element above the soundboard; the vibrating element of the instrument moves fastest at the moment of attack and gradually slows until the element stills, at which point, the sound ceases. Just as a player must come to understand and accept the limitations of the physical body to fully realize the anatomical possibilities of interacting with their instrument; the player must also, understand the physical limitations of their instrument. Once one comes to have a deep understanding of the strengths and limitations of both their instrument and their body, they are able to push the boundaries of creativity. Most extended techniques were created because the composer or performer understood the limitations of conventional playing methods and that allowed them to imagine new ways of interacting with the instrument. While, the piano and toy piano are physically limited in their conventional methods of sound production, it is important for the student musician to be aware of common articulation markings and their meanings; to promote a strong musical foundation, this book addresses frequently used articulations.

Symbol	Long Form Name	Description
	legato	long, connected playing,
	staccato	detached, short attack of notes
	tenuto	slightly stretched duration; in early music tradition where conventions were different, held for full value
	tie	used to indicate the sustain of two or more notes of the same pitch
	slur or phrase marking	used to denote a connection between notes of varied pitches
	marcato or accent	particular stress or emphasis on a specific note

CHAPTER EIGHT
RHYTHM STUDIES

Rhythm is area of music notation that deals with where on a given timeline a musical event occurs, whether that event is a sounding tone (**note**) or the absence of a sounding tone (**rest**). The following chapter introduces concepts of measured or metered time as it relates to notation and methods of counting. The student should be advised that while counting is helpful to the surface understanding of a piece, it is from fundamental rhythm where the subtlety and energy, which define the core of musicality, flow.

Simple meter
Beats can be broken into subdivisions of two

Simple Duple
Two beats per measure, which can be subdivided into two equal parts

2	Two quarter notes to each measure
4	Each quarter note subdivides into two eighth notes
2	Two half notes in each measure
2	Each half note subdivides into two quarter notes

Simple Triple
Three beats per measure

3	Three quarter notes per measure
4	Each quarter note subdivides into two eighth notes
3	Three whole notes per measure
1	Each whole note subdivides into two half notes

Compound meter
Beats can be subdivided in groups of three or other odd numbers such as five.

  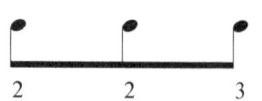

Compound duple
Two beats per measure, which are frequently, dotted values.

        6   Two dotted quarter notes per measure

        8   Each dotted quarter note subdivides into three eighth notes

Compound Triple
Three beats per measure.

        9   Three dotted quarter notes per measure

        8   Each dotted quarter note subdivides into three eighth notes

Compound Quadruple
Four beats per measure.

        12   Four dotted quarter notes per measure

        8   Each dotted quarter note subdivides into three eighth notes

General Rhythm Practice

Practice the following rhythm exercises.
Tap the rhythms on top of the toy piano, and remember to stay silent during the rests!

BEFORE YOU BEGIN COMPLETE THE FOLLOWING QUESTIONS FOR EACH EXERCISE!

1. *How many notes are in each measure?*
2. *What sort of note gets the beat?*
3. *Are the subdivisions of beat grouped in twos or threes?*
4. *Is this simple or compound meter?*
5. *Is the metronome set to the tempo marking indicated in the score?*

CHAPTER NINE
INTERVALS

Intervals

An **interval** is the distance between two notes. **Harmonic intervals** occur when two notes sound together, while **melodic intervals** are a measure the distance between two notes sounding in succession. Basic intervals can be labeled as more complex intervals by raising or lowering the pitch of the highest member of the interval, resulting in major, minor, augmented, and diminished intervals. All intervals are measured by the number of **half steps** (adjacent chromatic pitches) or **whole steps** (two neighboring chromatic pitches) above or below a given note. Basic intervals are measured from the lowest note to the highest note.

Unison

The simplest explanation for a unison is that a unison is the exact same note. For example, A3 and A3 are unisons. They are the same letter note and the same pitched note. On a single instrument this generally translates to a repetition of the note. In the case of playing two toy pianos unisons are generally not in tune with each other.

Second

The next interval in music is a second. A second occurs from one note to the next letter name in the cycle of the musical alphabet so for example D is a second above C. C and D-flat are also a second but in this case they are only a **half-step** or a **semitone** step away. C-natural to D-natural are a second as well in this case they are a **whole step** away from each other.

Third

The magical interval that makes up the basic foundation of Western functional tonality; it is the interval that builds a basic diatonic triad. It is... the mighty third! A major third is the product of four half steps above a given pitch, while a minor third is the product of three half steps. For example, a major third above C-natural is E-natural and the corresponding minor third above C-natural is E-flat.

Fourth

In early music, repetitions of fourths or fifths in composition were considered taboo. Today, quartal chords or harmonies built on the language of fourths rather than thirds create open sounding otherworldly textures, which (thanks to equal temperament) are quite pleasing to the modern ear. A perfect fourth is five half steps above the **fundamental tone** (original sounding pitch) and its taller awkward cousin the augmented fourth is the product of six half steps.

Fifth

The interval of the fifth is the next strongest member of the harmonic series following the octave, when a single note or fundamental is sounded. (When you play a C-Natural a hint of G-Natural is present as an overtone.) Playing the fifth and the fundamental together reinforces this organic relationship. The fifth is the third member of any common triad and akin to the fourth has been considered an open perfect interval. A perfect fifth is seven half steps away from the fundamental. For example, a fifth above C-Natural is G-Natural and the augmented cousin of that relationship is C-Natural to G-Sharp.

Sixth

The sixth is another of the consonant intervals, in the past when dissonance was avoided due to issues the peculiarities of early tunings it was a welcome element to composers writing for multiple voices because there are less rules about how to get into and out of harmony in sixths. It is also the diatonic pivot point for movement between major and minor scales bearing the same key signature. (Key signatures will be discussed in depth later in the text.) The major sixth is the product of nine half steps (C-Natural to A-Natural) while the minor sixth is spaced by eight half steps (C-Natural to A-Flat).

Seventh

The seventh has a strong relationship to the unison's cousin the octave. In composition, it is often referred to as the **leading tone** because it tends to "lead the ear" to the **tonic note** (the note for which a scale is named and around which **diatonic harmony** is centered) of a scale. The major seventh is formed by eleven half steps (C-Natural to B-Natural) while the minor seventh is ten half steps away from the fundamental pitch (C-Natural to B-Flat).

Octave

The octave is the final resting spot. It is the completion point of a full major or minor scale. It is the point at which the respelling of the musical alphabet returns. If one begins on C playing a full major or minor scale, they will end on the note C either an octave higher or lower than the one on which they began. An octave contains all twelve chromatic steps within the span of a pitch name (A3) to the next iteration of the pitch name on the keyboard (A4).

Ninth

The ninth is simply the interval of a second plus an octave. It is frequently used in jazz and while many of the smaller toy pianos may not incorporate this interval very often due to the limited range of the instrument, it is still helpful for the beginning musician to note for future studies.

Tenth

Another interval used to add color to common jazz language is the tenth and just like the ninth it is the product of a simple interval, in this case a third plus an octave. As mentioned in the previous section about the ninth, extended intervals are not a regular occurrence in every toy piano piece because of the varied sizes and ranges of toy pianos.

Inverting Intervals

In speaking of intervals, we often reference the relationship between a starting pitch and a note above the initial pitch; however, that relationship can be flipped or rather inverted. The name and quality of pitches (sharp, flat, or natural) does not change between the original interval and the inversion but the pitch class or where they sound on the instrument does. Inverting intervals is reliant upon the concept of octaves, previously discussed in this book, and the repetition of the musical alphabet. For these reasons, a third (C-Natural to E-Natural above) when inverted becomes a sixth (E-Natural below to C-Natural above). In the example, the C-Natural remains the same but E-Natural's relation above or below determines the final classification of the interval.

E is a third above C and also a sixth below C   **F is a fourth above C and also a fifth below C**

CHAPTER TEN
KEY SIGNATURES

Diatonic tonality

For years Western music has been based on the concept of **diatonic harmony**– that is harmony, which is created from the relationship of a seven-note scale plus the octave, where each letter of the scale represents a pitch adjacent to one another.

For example, an ascending C Major scale pans out in the following manner:

C   D   E   F   G   A   B   C

Three note chords called **triads** are created from the various degrees of the scale built in ascending thirds. (This does not account for chromatic alterations to chords, which composers use for various artistic reasons, as a visual artist blends paint on a palette.) Each chord built on a scale degree has a particular quality about it because of the relationships of the intervals of the third and fifth. The diatonic chords built on each scale degree have special names and qualities (major, minor, augmented, diminished).

Continuing our example with C Major:

Note Name	C	D	E	F	G	A	B	C
Scale Degree	1	2	3	4	5	6	7	8
Diatonic Chord	G	A	B	C	D	E	F	G
	E	F	G	A	B	C	D	E
Root in bold font	**C**	**D**	**E**	**F**	**G**	**A**	**B**	**C**
Diatonic Name	Tonic	Supertonic	Mediant	Subdominant	Dominant	Submediant	Leading Tone	Tonic

Diatonic Scales Mapped by Semitone

Major	W	W	H	W	W	W	H
Natural Minor	W	H	W	W	H	W	W
Melodic Minor							
Ascending	W	H	W	W	W	W	H
Descending	W	W	H	W	W	H	W
Harmonic Minor	W	H	W	W	H	A2	H

H = Half Step or Semitone   W = Whole Step   A2 = Augmented Second

41

Circle of Fifths

Key signatures were invented to reduce the usage of ink made in repeating the same diatonic accidentals in a piece. The accidentals, which are common to a key, are placed at the beginning of the staff so that the player knows that the accidental applies unless otherwise cancelled by a different accidental. For example, in the key of D Major has two accidentals, F-sharp and C-sharp, two sharps are placed on the staff line and space corresponding to those notes meaning that every F or C the player sees in the score will be an F# or C#. In a time where ink and paper were costly and took a good while to make, the key signature was a valuable invention.

The addition of accidentals, whether flat or sharp, for the series of key signatures in the musical language follows the interval of a fifth. C Major which also bears the same key signature as A Minor having no accidentals, starts the circle; moving to the right one sharp is added, which denotes the key signatures of G Major and E Minor and the cycle continues. Both a diagram of the circle of fifths and a key signature chart have been included in this text for your reference.

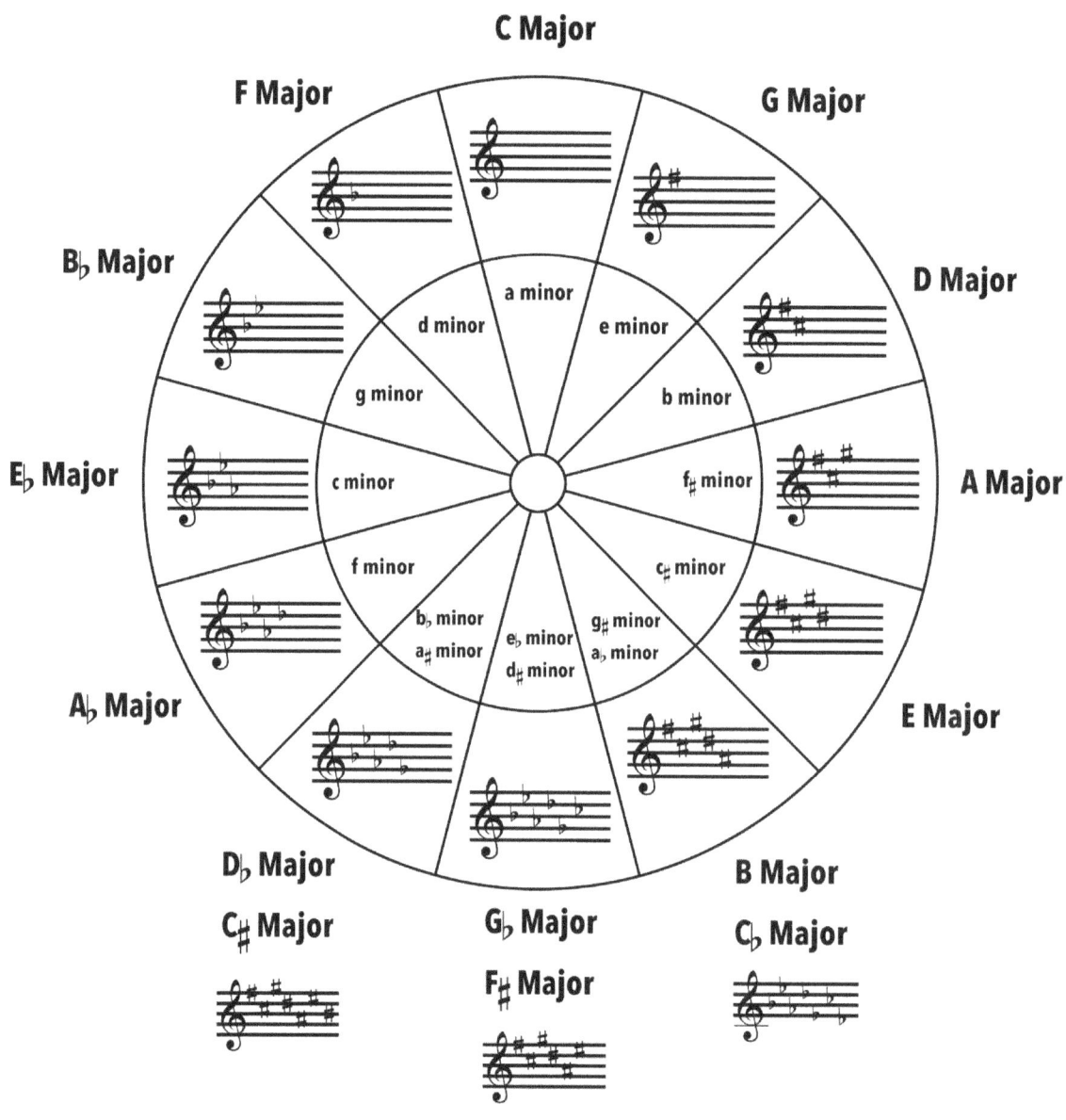

CHAPTER ELEVEN
SCALES

A scale in the simplest definition is a set of notes in an ascending or descending sequence with adjacent pitches following the musical alphabet. Scales are a vital part of learning and maintaining technical skill on any instrument. It is a normal expectation for professional pianists to be able to play through four octaves of any scale at a quick and even pace; a task that is made possible because the traditional piano has 88-keys a range big enough to enable this feat of agility. The toy piano in contrast has a maximum of 37-keys and this book has been written for the Schoenhut 25-key tabletop model toy piano. For this reason, rather than focusing on the full seven note major or minor scales, we will concern ourselves with what are known as pentachord scales, which outline the first five notes of the larger major as well as minor scales. ***A comprehensive list of scales is located in the exercise section at the back of the book.***

BEFORE YOU PRACTICE A SCALE CONSIDER THE FOLLOWING QUESTIONS!

1. What does the key signature say?
2. Which notes are sharp or flat?
3. What is the recommended fingering?
4. What tempo should I set my metronome for practice?
5. Am I in the optimal relaxed playing position?

C Major

C Natural Minor

C Harmonic Minor

C Melodic Minor

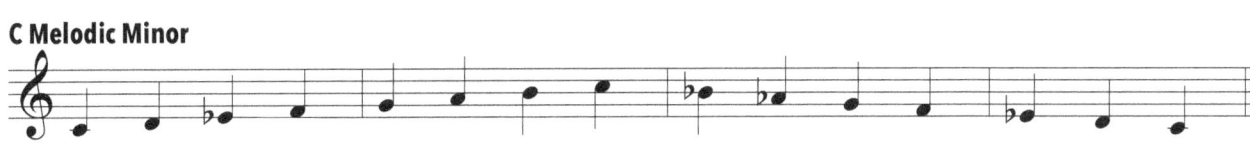

CHAPTER TWELVE
CHORDS

A **chord** is a collection of three or more pitches sounded at the same time, or interpreted for analytical purposes as sounding at the same time. The most common chord is a diatonic triad a chord, built in thirds and has members that belong exclusively to the key signature without chromatic alteration. **Chord progression**, is the term given to the succession of chords in a given piece or section of music. A progression may or may not repeat or follow a cycle.

Triad Chord Qualities

A **triad** is a chord with three members spaced a third apart in root position. Triads come in several different shades depending on the distance between chord members: major, minor, augmented, and diminished. A **major triad** is made up of four semitones between the root and the third (or second member of the chord and the middle voice in root position) and eight semitones between the root and the fifth (highest member of the chord in root position). A **minor triad** is made up of three semitones between the root and the third and eight semitones between the root and the fifth. An **augmented triad** is made up of four semitones between the root and the third and nine semitones between the root and the fifth. A **half-diminished triad** is made up of four semitones between the root and the third and seven semitones between the root and the fifth. A **fully diminished triad** is made up of three semitones between the root and the third and seven semitones between the root and the fifth.

Playing Methods

Blocked
All members of the chord are played simultaneously.

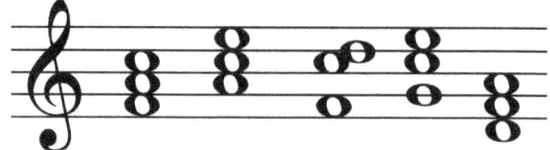

Arpeggio
An Italian word meaning "broken," arpeggiating a chord simply means to play one member (sometimes two members in particularly complex passages) of the chord at a time.

Alberti Bass Pattern

Before the invention of the modern piano, early keyboard instruments did not have the ability to sustain for long periods of time. The modern toy piano shares this limitation with its early music predecessors. To keep the harmony moving through the acoustic space many early musicians took to arpeggiating left hand figures. **Alberti Bass** is a specific pattern for three pitch chords played in the following order: lowest, highest, middle, highest. The name Alberti Bass comes from the 18th century composer Domenico Alberti, who frequently used the technique in his works.

Inverting Chords

Just as intervals can be inverted through respelling because the musical alphabet repeats through octaves, chords can also be inverted. Basic triads have a **root position**, where all the notes are spelled in thirds, which sit directly on top of one another with the lowest note being the root note of the chord. Following the root position, there is **first inversion**, where the second chord member is now the lowest in the spelling of the chord. The final inversion of a triad, called **second inversion**, places the third member of the triad (which would be a fifth above the root note in root position) at the bottom of the chord, with the other members above it.

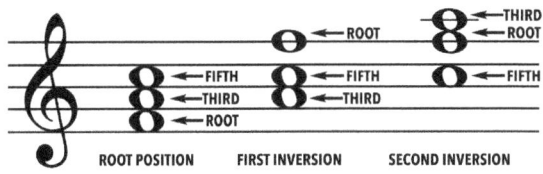

Quartal & Quintal Chords

Most of the Western musical tradition is based on chords built in thirds called triads, but as composers tried to innovate musical language and push the boundaries of textural possibility they began to build chords and tonal language based on the intervals of the fourth and fifth. **Quartal chords** have three or more members, and in root position all members of the chord are a fourth apart from the nearest subsequent chord member. **Quintal chords** have three or more members, and in root position all members of the chord are a fifth apart from the nearest subsequent chord member.

Quintal Chords

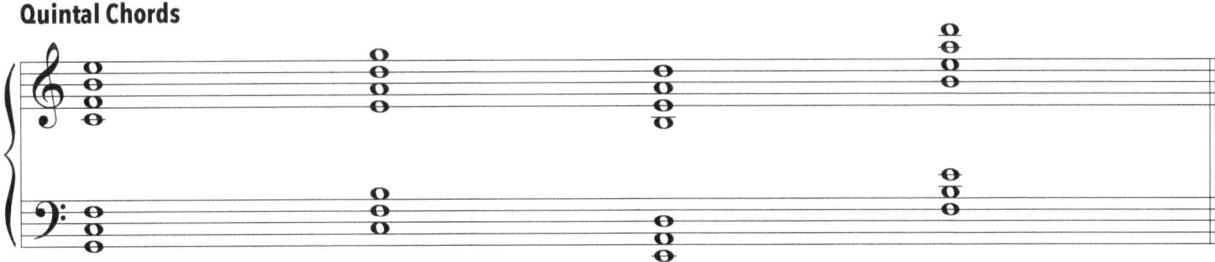

Quartal Chords

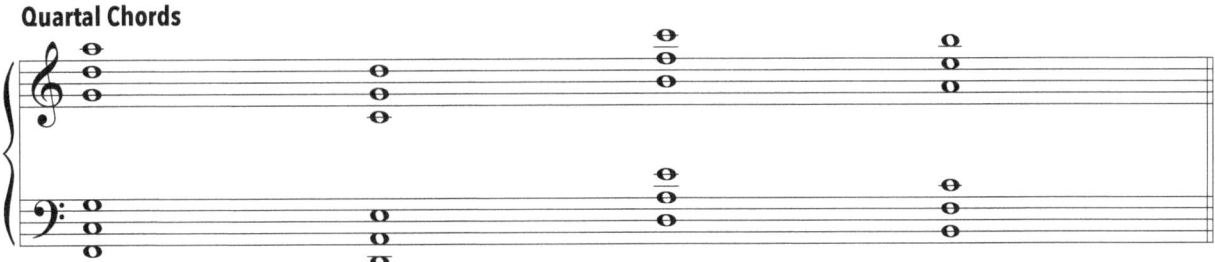

CHAPTER THIRTEEN
TRANSPOSITION

Transposition is the act of taking musical material and moving it from one key center to another. In transposition from minor key to minor key or Major key to Major key, intervals both melodic and harmonic maintain their integrity while, the whole phrase moves up or down in relation to the new tonal center. Transposing from major to minor keys involves a few more complications just since the intervals within the major and minor scales differ, and while we won't focus heavily on complex transposition in this book, the student should know that transposition from major to minor or minor to major is a possibility. The skill of being able to transpose a passage at sight is valuable for all musicians. It is particularly useful to be able to transpose at sight when accompanying a singer, who might bring a score in a key that doesn't suit his or her natural range.

Original Excerpt in C minor

Excerpt Transposed to E minor

Excerpt Transposed to C Major

PRACTICE AND PERFORMANCE

CHAPTER FOURTEEN
PRACTICE

The journey to becoming a proficient musician would not exist without a serious dedication to practicing one's instrument. Many traditional method books focus on repertoire or studies for the student to practice *ad nauseum* and eventually the student reaches a plateau where the inspiration to learn an instrument gives way to boredom and frustration. This text is designed to keep the learner engaged by targeting a number of subjects along the path to toy piano proficiency from music history to music theory to solo repertoire and studies. Practice comes naturally to some artists but for many musicians and hobbyists, learning how to practice is essential to the enjoyment of performing on a musical instrument whether it is for a crowd of a thousand people or an intimate concert in one's living room for the family cats.

Preparation
A common complaint of students first learning an instrument is that they "don't know what to practice" or "how long to practice." Musical practice requires a lot of concentration because the musician's brain must process and send a great deal of information in almost an instant: a pianist must interpret the notes on the page and then translate to a physical location on the playing field, at the same time they have to analyze the rhythms and anticipate what is coming next in the score. One can't play a rhythm of two quarter notes if they can't time the impulse of the second quarter note. The fine motor skills that allow a pianist to bring out a melody and provide more weight to a single note or musical line while maintaining a consistent background with other notes under this spotlighted section are another source of complication. The student musician should not be deterred by what can sometimes look like a Mount Everest to climb. An old African proverb offers wise advice for anyone seeking to learn music:

> ***How does one eat an elephant?***
>
> ***One bite at a time...***

This concept is crucial to the planning of practice time. The student should develop a list of goals for each practice session. That list looks considerably different from playing level to playing level and session-to-session. As for length of practice time that will vary, the student must gauge how long they can successfully focus on a specific practice task before their concentration level starts to wane at which point the student should take a break or move on to another task. For instance, Riley is working diligently on a new solo piece but is having problems getting past the measure eight because it presents some challenging rhythms which Riley has not seen before. She keeps practicing the same mistakes and continues growing frustrated until she remembers one of her practice goals for this session was to master the C Major scale at 160 BPM. Riley decides to put her solo piece away for fifteen minutes while she works on her scales and arpeggios. When she finishes practicing her scales she moves on to spot practicing measure eight.

A written rundown of what the student intends to tackle also does a great deal to prevent a practice plateau. Practice plans should reinforce the things, which the student has already learned but should also present a new skill or new section of a performance work. **It should be noted that a practice plan is separate from a warm-up routine**. Practice plans and routines may for instance, both include scales such as F Major or c minor; however, the difference is that in a routine, the primary objective is to get the body moving, much like an athlete doing a jog before practice, the scales serve to get the blood flowing; whereas a practice plan is akin to the football players running specific plays out of a playbook. So, the musician in their practice plan takes the F Major scale and works on something finite such as varying articulations or tempo or phrasing. The companion exercise book for this text comes with a musician's practice planner to assist students in developing effective and positive practice habits.

Technical Studies	*Repertoire*	*Improvisation/Free Study*
Scales – Legato at 85 BPM (C Major, a minor) **Chords** – Inversions of diatonic chords (C Major, a minor)	**Seventh Interval Study - Harmonic Dream (1991)** Measures 1-10 Spot practice measure 11	Improvisation on the theme of water without using arpeggios
Time Spent: _____	**Time Spent:** _____	**Time Spent:** _____

Spot Practicing

Spot practicing can cut down considerably on frustration and is an exceptionally efficient way to practice. An advanced musician, knowing their own weaknesses, can look at a score and target the tough sections from the first read-through and a wise practicing musician will mark these sections for spot practice. Beginner and intermediate musicians generally play through until they come to a difficult part, at which point they should circle the problematic section. Remembering the wisdom about eating an elephant, the student should isolate the smallest unit of the problematic section, usually this is a single short rhythmic moment about half of a measure. The student very slowly (half-tempo or less) should practice this small moment until they can reliably play the figure ten times in a row with no mistakes. Once the half-measure moment has been mastered at the slow tempo, the student should seek to add the moment into the full measure, still remembering to practice slowly and seeking to play the full measure correctly at least ten times in a row. Once the full measure has been mastered, the student should add the measure prior to the problematic measure into the repetition cycle and after that two-measure cycle has been mastered the student should add the measure after the spotlight measure into the cycle. When the student can confidently play the three-measure cycle at the slow tempo and after gradually bringing the three-measure cycle up to the tempo of the piece, the student may proceed to re-integrate the spotted section into the full piece.

Spot practicing is important to maintaining the flow of a piece in performance. When a memory slip happens the mistake that caused the player to forget what happens next in the piece, frequently occurs earlier in the work prior to the catastrophic end of the fundamental rhythm. Such breaks in memory, which disturb the organic unfolding of a composition, are preventable by slow focused practice with special attention or spot work on the tough sections of the piece.

Slow Practice

Practicing at a slow tempo with focus and purpose is essential to the smooth and seamless performance of music. During slow practice it is much easier to spot and correct a problem than in rushed practice. Emphasis on slow practice does not mean that a musician should refrain from playing things at tempo, after the passage has been successfully mastered at a slow tempo, the musician should seek to gradually push the tempo, so that when the piece is at the composer's/artist's desired tempo the performer has not lost control, musicality, or relaxed playing technique to the faster iteration of the composition. Slow practice is integral to getting the mind and body in sync, which is fundamental to translating the dots on a page or the music one hears in their heart/mind into reality in a flowing cohesive manner.

It should be noted however, that exhaustive slow practice is no guarantee for perfect playing at high tempos. The movement and coordination required when playing exceptionally fast or virtuosic passages means that one must work on the fine motor skills and speed to move from place to place along the playing plane. Once the notes and rhythms have been extracted from the page and mastered at a slow speed, and the passage has been committed to memory (a key component in fast playing, because the average player does not have the ability to accurately sight read exceptionally complex and fast passages) the student should begin to increase the tempo at which they practice the passage. It is advisable as well to practice fast passages above and below the tempo, as one should never feel out of control when playing particularly in performance. In the modern era of YouTube where there seems to be a push to see how fast one can play a piece because the visual impact often supersedes the auditory value, something very important has been lost; at some point one sacrifices musicality to speed because they are playing on the edge of what is possible and because at some point the notes are flying by so quickly that they become a blur to the brain… a technique that may be used by composer for effect in a modern work but outside of an intended effect, one should never seek to play a work faster than he or she can interpret the work with some musical sensitivity.

Note Taking

Brief pauses during practice time to write reminders or notes in one's score are an important part of the learning process. There's a lot to recall when learning a piece and while learning an instrument, a short note such as "louder here" or "faster here" are of particular assistance because it puts things in plain language for the student. One should always have a notebook and pencil handy in their practice space. If the student is working with a professional teacher having notes from practice sessions provides for focused lessons, which is great because private music lessons are often expensive.

Critique & Review

Practice time does not end when the last note of the last work is played. At least five to ten minutes should be devoted to reviewing what improvements were made during the session as well as what aspects of technical playing or the current repertoire need work. A mirror in the practice space is of tremendous assistance for checking that proper posture and relaxed hand techniques are being applied. Another very useful tool for modern practice is a smartphone or other camera device. Recording one's practice sessions and then taking the time to review the video will reveal a host of issues that need attention but it will also highlight a number of improvements and accomplishments that one is making on their journey as a music student.

CHAPTER FIFTEEN
IMPROVISATION

Improvisation is not part of the traditional piano method and short of studying jazz's stylized improvisatory language there is no guide for the student musician. Improvisation has a world of interpretations as vast as the possibilities it affords a musician. Previously, in this book the concept of structured improvisation was introduced, as music, which is produced based on a set of material ranging from extra-musical concepts to a set of pitches to specific harmonic language, text instructions, and anything that a composer-performer collaboration can brainstorm ahead of a performance. The improvisatory element in structured improvisation, therefore, comes when the performer, having been presented with a set of parameters ahead of the performance, creates a new musical work that is unique to the time and space in which it is created. In theory, structured improvisation works could be painstakingly notated and replicated but there is something magical about improvisation that has a special energy away from strictly notated music. The music of our ancestors before the advent of notation was improvisatory and perhaps there is a deep-seated primal connection to music breaks or works which stray from grid-based robotic music of the modern world. There are a number of different ways to think about improvisation and while, each artist comes to develop their own system for improvisation, which forms a "signature sound," there are a few different approaches to improvisation that can serve as a jumping off point for the student musician. It is important to remember that while each of these approaches is introduced separately, they often do and should overlap in the course of an improvisatory musical performance.

Harmonic
The first method of improvisation is the one that is primarily used in pop, jazz, gospel, and other forms of music that rely on a set chord progression. The musician uses the notes included within the chord progression (sometimes with chromatic embellishments) that follows the rules of diatonic harmony. For example, if a pianist reading a lead sheet has the progression centered around the chords synonymous with the key of E-minor the improvisation will likely take liberties with the E-minor scale and might dance in and out of G-Major, the **relative major key** of E-minor.

Linear
In the modern musical world improvisation is not always set in or around a particular key, instead a collection of pitches, which may or may not conform to traditional melodic contour are the basis of improvisation. Sometimes composers will notate specific pitches and pitch classes to be used for a predetermined length of time, which is often notated within the score.

Textural
Another approach to improvisation is from the viewpoint of texture. In this style, the primary concert is not specific notes or harmonies but rather the density of notes (how closely one note is followed by another or how many notes sound simultaneously) and the articulation of notes (how quick is the attack of a note, additionally, how quickly does the sound go away).

Dynamic
Similar to textural improvisation, dynamic improvisation is concerned with contrast. Since dynamics are concerned with how loud or soft sound can be, dynamic improvisation, exploits these crests and troughs. Musicians who are particularly astute with judging the acoustics of a room can push the sound pressure levels to the brink of audience discomfort and immediately sink into the near silence of the natural noise floor. The effect is that the loud makes the soft seem softer and the soft makes the loud seem louder.

Text
Improvisation based on text can be as specific or ambiguous as the composer or performance collective decide for it to be. For example, a composer may create an index of possible sounds or extended techniques that they want the performer to use. In some cases, the text improvisation may require the performer to actually speak or sing from written text in the score. The commonality in text improvisation is that there is some predefined structure set forth by instructions for the performer.

Concept
Like musical charades, concept improvisation uses an extra-musical idea such as rain, love, earthquake, magic, or a host of other ideas as a jumping off point for musical creation. It is structured, in that the musician is expected to create a sound painting, which evokes the mental picture of the concept or object at hand; but it is free, in that, those specific musical techniques and sounds used to create that aural image are left to the discretion of the performer.

Free
Improvisation, having no predefined structure or format is free. Sometimes the case is made that jazz works having no tonal center or written beginnings are free improvisations. Free improvisation is generally reserved to classify avant-garde and experimental works, which create and maintain a musical language individual to that specific work at that specific time. Of all forms of improvisation, free improvisation is the most difficult to notate. It relies heavily on a strong internal system and expression of musical feeling, and in-group settings requires delving into an unspoken connection with other players where one "senses" the energy of the others around them.

Group vs. Solo
Solo improvisation requires the musician to be in touch with their internal organic musical tendencies but group improvisation has more demands. When improvising within an ensemble, each player has a responsibility to the musicians to listen attentively to what each person is adding to the group. A common faux pas of young improvisers is that they play too much and that quintessential musical conversation between members of the ensemble is lost. It is the musical equivalent of the annoying dinner guest who interrupts everyone's stories with hour-long tales about their life. What happens when one is an active listener in an improvising ensemble is that one notices linear, rhythmic, harmonic, textural, and dynamic material that can be used as a jumping off point for more material during the performance. Trading these themes and musical objects throughout the ensemble add a sense of cohesion, which is comforting to the audience. When one listens to a piece of music the brain is working to predict what comes next, when the music subverts the expected outcome, the brain can either become frustrated or delighted. Even the most complex 20th century post-tonal musical has some cohesion, the issue is that not many

of us have worked to develop a long musical comprehension; however, if one were to stop and analyze many of these "unlistenable" works, one would find patterns and pitches that relate to the material at the very beginning of the piece.

In the end, improvisation is a skill that comes as one becomes more confident in their abilities to play their instrument as well as the comfort level to communicate with other musicians without spoken prompts. The more one practices, the more one is willing to put themselves out there, the more one learns about what works and doesn't work for them. It is the synthesis of all these improvisational experiences that ultimately allows one to define their signature sound and personal system of improvisation.

APPENDICES

CIRCLE OF FIFTHS

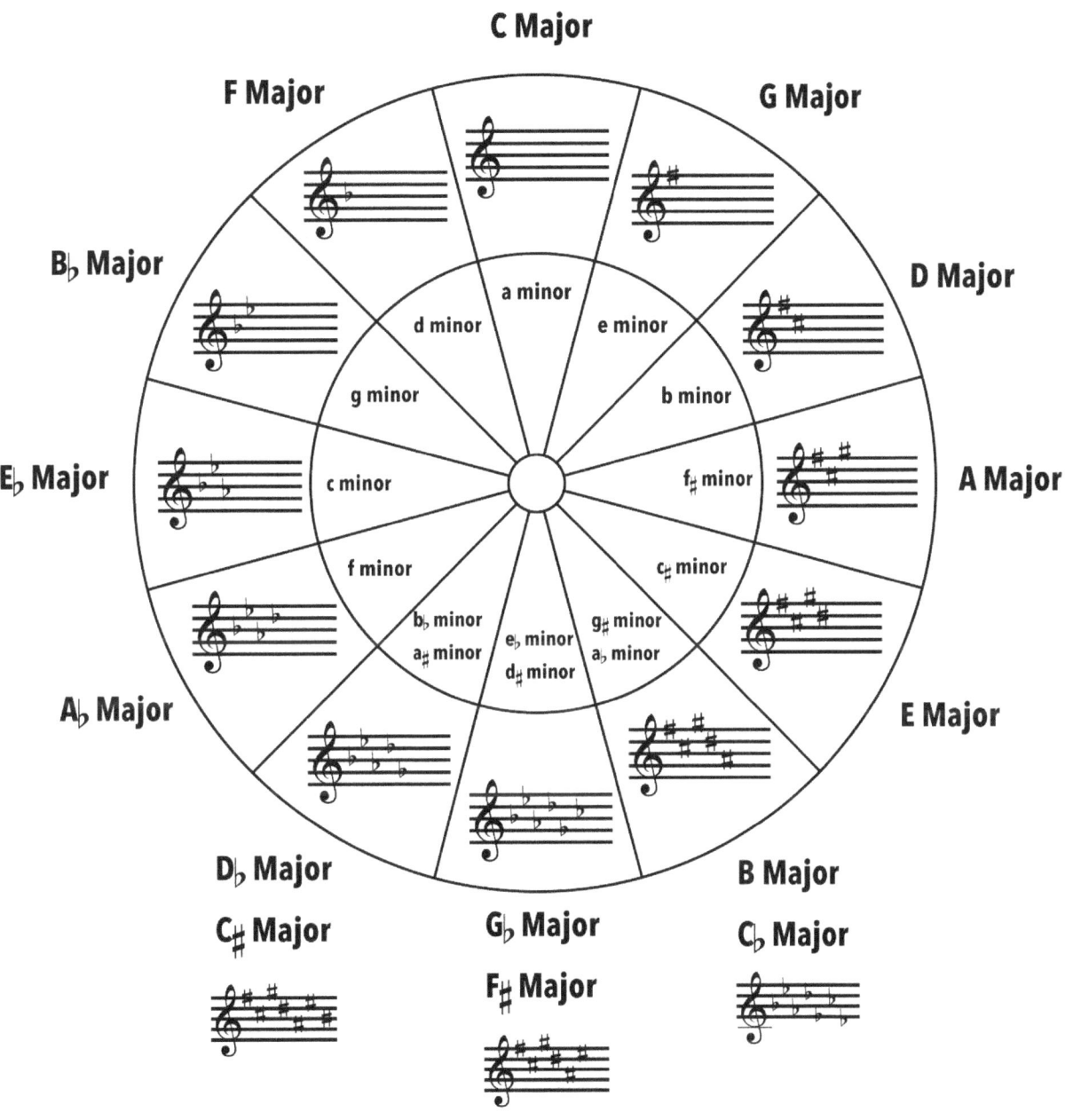

DIATONIC CHORD CHART

C MAJOR

Note Name	C	D	E	F	G	A	B	C
Scale Degree	1	2	3	4	5	6	7	8
Diatonic Chord *Root in bold*	G E **C**	A F **D**	B G **E**	C A **F**	D B **G**	E C **A**	F D **B**	G E **C**
Diatonic Name	Tonic	Supertonic	Mediant	Subdominant	Dominant	Submediant	Leading Tone	Tonic

C Major

C Natural Minor

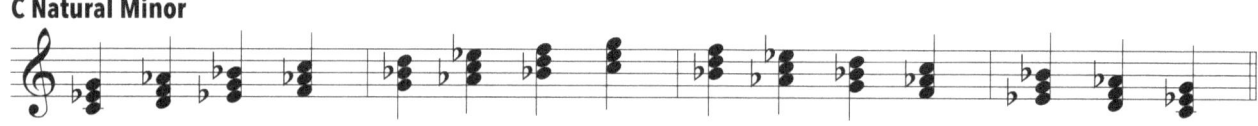

C Harmonic Minor

C Melodic Minor

DYNAMICS CHART

Symbol	Long Form Name	Dynamic Value
pp	pianissimo	very soft
p	piano	soft
mp	mezzo piano	medium soft
mf	mezzo forte	medium loud
f	forte	loud
ff	fortissimo	very loud

FINGERING CHART

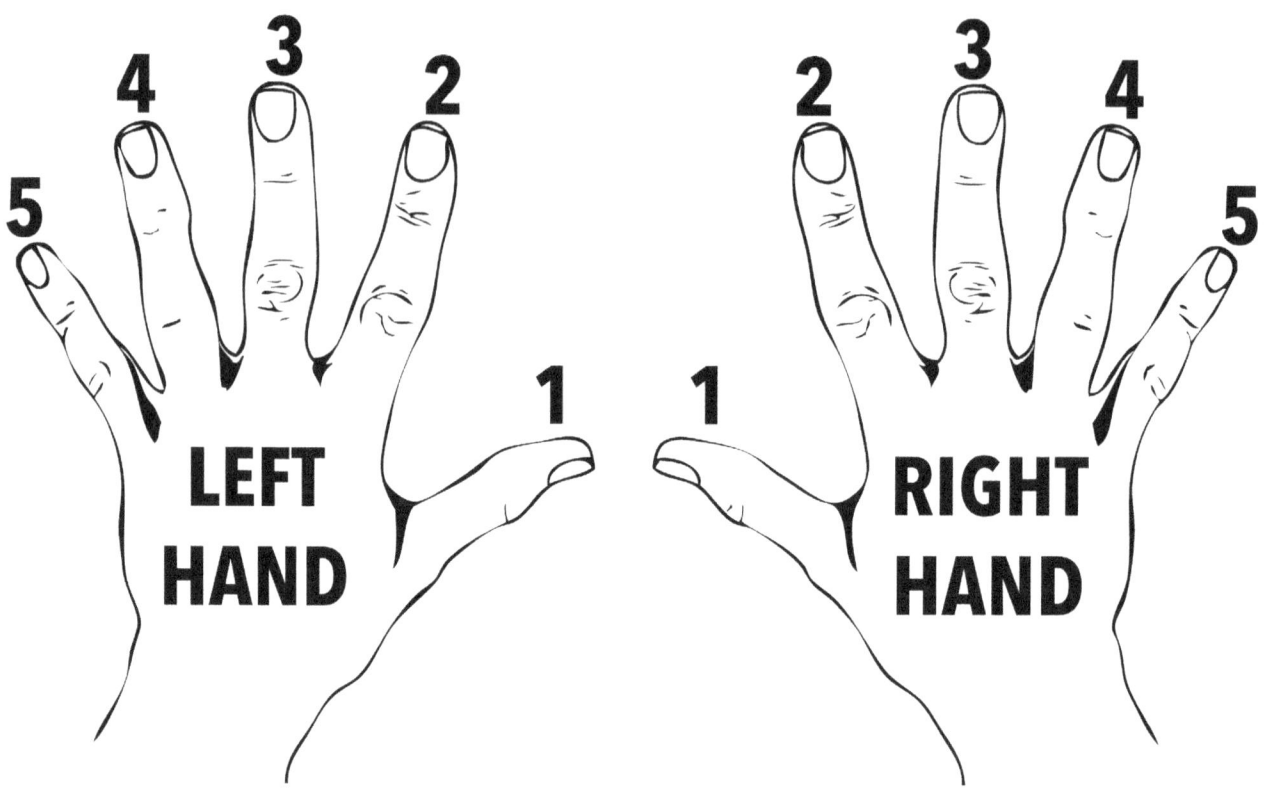

KEY SIGNATURE CHART

KEYBOARD DIAGRAM

ACCIDENTALS ON THE KEYBOARD

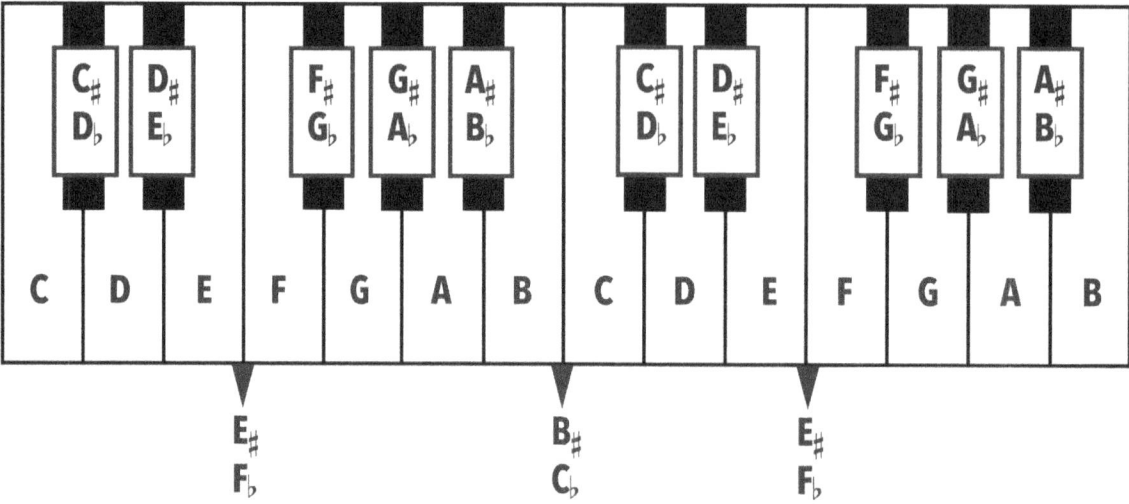

RHYTHM CHART

Whole Note	𝅝	4 beats	**Whole Rest**	▬	4 beats
Half Note	𝅗𝅥	2 beats	**Half Rest**	▬	2 beats
Quarter Note	♩	1 beat	**Quarter Rest**	𝄽	1 beat
Eighth Note	♪	½ beat	**Eighth Rest**	𝄾	½ beat
Sixteenth Note	𝅘𝅥𝅯	¼ beat	**Sixteenth Rest**	𝄿	¼ beat
Dotted Whole Note	𝅝.	6 beats	**Dotted Whole Rest**	▬.	6 beats
Dotted Half Note	𝅗𝅥.	3 beats	**Dotted Half Rest**	▬.	3 beats
Dotted Quarter Note	♩.	1 ½ beat	**Dotted Quarter Rest**	𝄽.	1 ½ beat

TEMPO CHART

BPM Examples

♩ = 120   𝅗𝅥 = 60   ♪ = 144

Common Italian Markings

Grave	Very slow	25-45 BPM
Largo	Broadly	40-60 BPM
Adagio	Stately and with ease	66-70 BPM
Andante	At a walking pace	76-108 BPM
Moderato	Moderately	108-120 BPM
Allegro	Fast, bright	120-168 BPM
Vivace	Fast and lively	168-176 BPM
Presto	Very fast	168-200 BPM

Tempo Alterations

Ritardando	Gradual slow in tempo	Abbreviation: rit.
Accelerando	Speeding up gradually	Abbreviation: accel.
a tempo	Back to the original tempo	
Rubato	Freedom to adjust the tempo for artistic interpretation	

TREBLE CLEF & STAFF

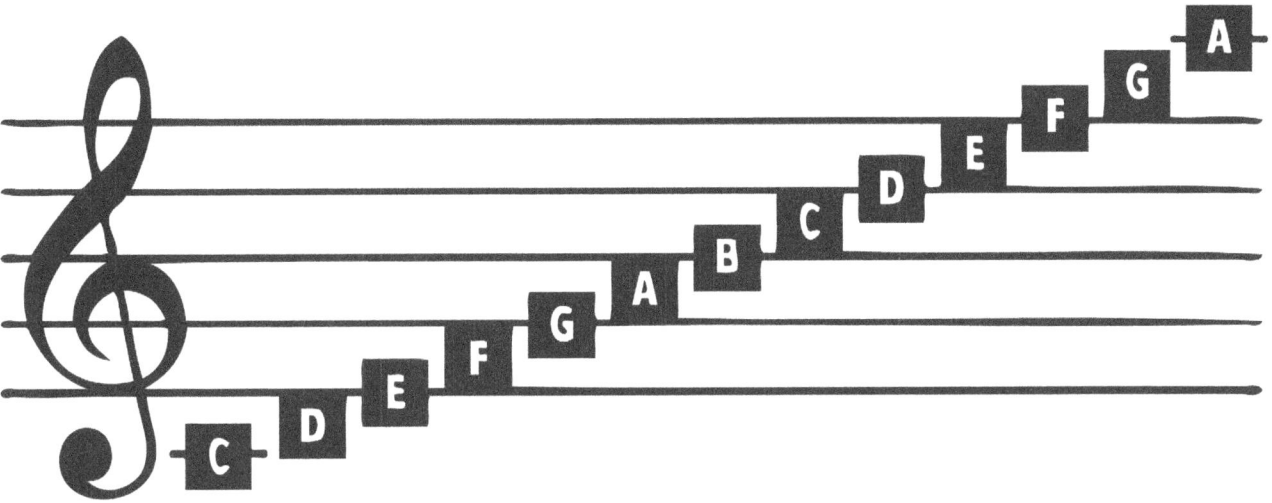

GLOSSARY

accidental - any symbol used to represent the raising or lowering of a pitch by one or two half steps; also used to cancel a previous pitch alteration or part of a key signature

Alberti bass - 18th century left-hand keyboard pattern used to maintain harmony to compensate for the short acoustic sustain of early keyboard instruments

arpeggio - an Italian word meaning broken; in music it is used to describe any figure where the members of a chord are played in succession

avant-garde music - works created outside of the conventional Western harmonic language either in concept or presentation

baroque - Western music period from the end of the 16th Century to the death of Bach in 1750; began with homophonic textures of the Renaissance style and ended with a intense exploration of polyphonic writing known as counterpoint which had strict rules governing voice leading or part-writing

chord - a collection of three or more pitches played together or interpreted as being played together for the purposes of harmonic analysis of a musical work

chromatic - the scale containing all twelve half step divisions of the octave; a pitch outside of the key signature added to a harmony or melodic passage

classical music - the body of works created between the early-18th and late-19th century particularly stylized by the First Viennese School (Beethoven, Haydn, Mozart, Schubert) and subsequent music written in this clearly defined style; in popular vernacular any music of a "serious" nature

compound meter - time signature or meter that has a subdivision of three

concert pitch - the reference pitch used by orchestras and chamber groups for performance; in America the standard tuning pitch is A-440, while in Europe the standard tuning pitch varies between A-442 and A-445

diatonic - the collection of pitches and associated harmonies that are a natural part of a key without any chromatic alterations

dynamic marking - a symbol, written word, or explicit instructions detailing how loud or soft to play

electroacoustic music - music which uses some form of electronic media whether fixed or interactive in conjunction with a live performer on an acoustic instrument which may or may not be amplified

electronic music - music made using digital processing or analog synthesis

equal temperament - the prevailing system of tuning in the Western music tradition which splits the octave into twelve equal parts; the tuning system which allows for easy movement between keys and chromatic language

experimental music - works created outside of the conventional Western harmonic language either in concept or presentation

extended techniques - any method of playing an instrument or vocal production beyond Western conventional means; for example, a pianist strumming the strings inside a piano, a percussionist using a cello bow on a vibraphone, or a singer employing throat singing methods of the Far East

figured bass - early system of keyboard notation using numbers underneath the bass line to indicate harmonic intervals for accompaniment

fixed media - pre-recorded or pre-processed audio that may be presented as a standalone work or can be used as part of an electroacoustic performance with a live performer

found object - something fashioned to be used as a musical instrument that is "discovered" or "happened upon" this includes broken instruments found in thrift stores or the garbage as well as common household items repurposed for musical means

free improvisation - music created without a predefined structure or written score

graphic notation - musical notation using visual elements outside of the standard notation tradition, such as photos, cartoons, charts, and others

half-step - the smallest division within an octave in the Western tuning system of equal temperament; also referred to as a semitone

harmonic interval - the distance between two notes sounded simultaneously

harmonic series - the collection of overtones naturally occurring in a single pitch or fundamental tone

harmony - typically attributed to the Western concept of functional tonality; the relationship between pitches sounding simultaneously, or for the purposes of analysis, are interpreted as sounding simultaneously

improvisation - music created in real time that is not a note-for-note realization of a written score

interval - the distance between two pitches

inversion - (*intervals*) the complementary relationship between two pitches when one is displaced by an octave; for example, the third C-Natural to E-Natural when reflected around the C-Natural becomes a sixth with E-Natural as the lower member of the interval *(chords)* related by virtue of having the same members, but these may be displaced by octave so that the root of the chord is no longer the lowest sounding member of the chord

jazz standard - a common work in the repertoire which is often reduced to a simplified score called a lead sheet, from which musicians interpret a specific theme and improvise over a given chord progression

live electronics - real time computer or synthesized processing of audio

melodic interval - the distance between two notes sounding in succession

melody - pitches in succession which form a definable line musically whether by relationship of frequency, rhythmic motive, diatonic harmony, or pantonal harmony

overtone – members of the harmonic series that are included when a pitch or fundamental tone sounds which are not as strong as the fundamental tone and serve to color the pitch

pantonal – a type of tonality or musical language in which the hierarchy of pitches synonymous to diatonic harmony is replaced with a system where all chromatic pitches are considered equal

pitch - the frequency of a note or fundamental tone

pitch class - refers to the specific octave of a note or fundamental tone

scale - a set of notes in an ascending or descending sequence with adjacent pitches following the musical alphabet

semitone - the smallest division within an octave in the Western tuning system of equal temperament; also referred to as a half step

simple meter - time signature or meter that has a subdivision of three

staff - the system of lines and spaces upon which music is notated

structured improvisation - music created in real time based on predefined parameters but not a note-for-note realization of a written score

tempo - the rate at which a piece of music is played; the rate may fluctuate throughout the piece according to instruction from the composer; may be measured in finite time using a specific rate of beats per minute (BPM)

text notation - directions for performance, which are written out in lieu of traditional music notation on a staff system

time signature - sign at the beginning of a composition as well as within a composition, at the discretion of the composer, which informs the player of how many beats are in a measure and which rhythmic value gets the beat

tine - a metal bar that is tuned and produces musical sound by striking or bowing the bar

tonality - concerned with the Western rules and preferences centered around diatonic harmony

toy piano - a miniature version the traditional 88-key piano, which uses a series of graduated pitched metal bars called tines in lieu of strings to produce sound; originally designed for children's study, the instrument has found a place on the modern concert stage as a serious instrument in both ensembles for effect as well as for solo performance

treble clef - also called the "G-Clef" because it encircles the "G" line of the standard staff, it is used to reference the pitches above middle-C

whole step - the second smallest division of an octave; two semitones equal one whole step

WRITTEN EXERCISES

THE STAFF - LINES

Lines on the staff are counted from the bottom to the top, on which line of the staff is the dot?

LINE 2

THE STAFF – SPACES

Spaces on the staff are counted from the bottom to the top, on which space of the staff is the dot?

SPACE 1

THE STAFF – LINES & SPACES

Place a circle on the line or space indicated by the text.

| LINE 4 | SPACE 1 | LINE 1 | LINE 5 | SPACE 4 |

| SPACE 2 | LINE 3 | LINE 2 | SPACE 2 | SPACE 3 |

| LINE 1 | SPACE 4 | SPACE 1 | LINE 4 | LINE 5 |

| LINE 3 | LINE 2 | SPACE 3 | LINE 1 | SPACE 2 |

THE STAFF – LEDGER LINES

Identify the number of the line or space indicated by the dot on the ledger line.

Draw the necessary ledger lines and place a dot on the line or space indicated by the text.

BAR LINES - IDENTIFICATION

Identify the type of bar line and describe what it indicates.

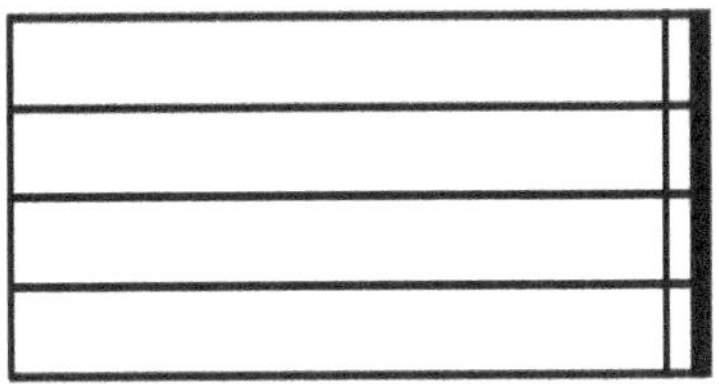

Type: _____

Description: _____

_____

_____

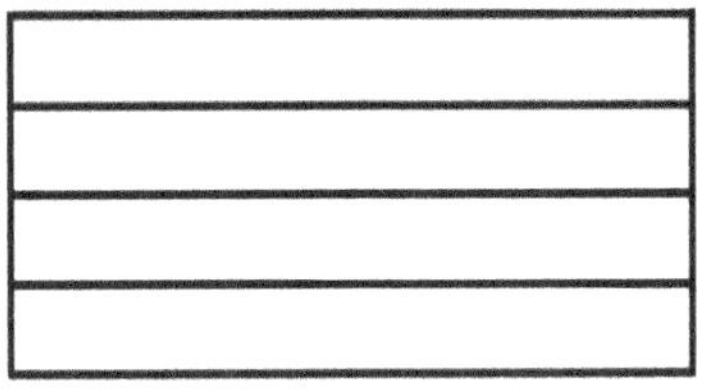

Type: _____

Description: _____

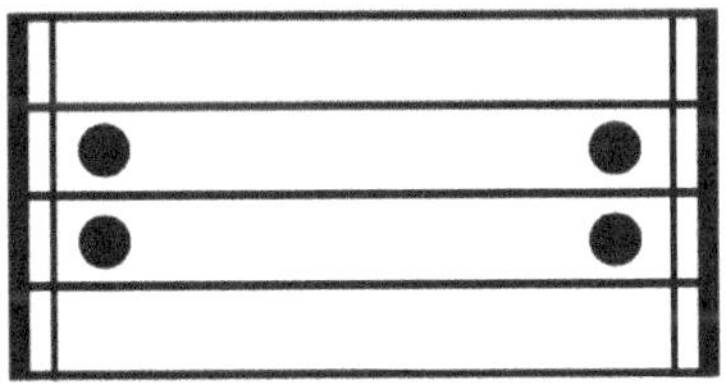

_____

_____

Type: _____

Description: _____

_____

_____

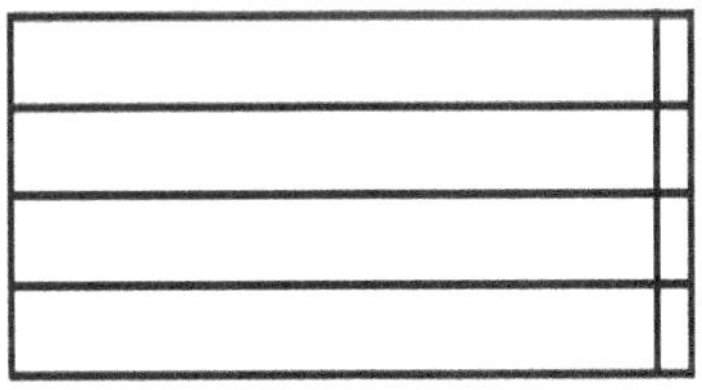

Type: _____

Description: _____

_____

_____

Draw a left bar line to the left of the measure, which indicates the end of a section.

Draw a bar line to the left of the measure, which indicates the end of a piece.

Draw a bar line to the left and right of the measure, which indicates the repeat of a section.

TREBLE CLEF - DRAWING

Draw treble clefs using the space provided.

Draw treble clefs on the staves below. Remember to make sure they encircle the second line of staff.

TREBLE CLEF - LINES

What is the pitch name of the indicated note?

D

TREBLE CLEF - SPACES

What is the pitch name of the indicated note?

F

TREBLE CLEF – PITCH IDENTIFICATION

Name the pitch indicated on the staff. Draw a treble clef to make sure your identification is correct

Draw the pitch identified by the text. Draw a treble clef before you draw the note.

| C | A | G | E | B |

| F | A | C | E | G |

| B | G | D | F | A |

| E | D | A | C | B |

COMMON NOTES

Draw whole notes using the space provided.

Draw half notes using the space provided.

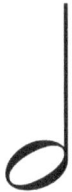

Draw quarter notes using the space provided.

Draw eighth notes using the space provided.

Draw sixteenth notes using the space provided.

Draw the note indicated by the number of beats.

| 1 BEAT | 1/2 BEAT | 2 BEATS | 4 BEATS |

| 2 BEATS | 4 BEATS | 1 BEAT | 1/2 BEAT |

Draw the specified note on the staff, making sure that the center of the note head is on the line or space indicated by the text. Indicated the number of the line or space where the pitch is located. You will need to draw a treble clef and you may need to draw ledger lines to complete this exercise. Use A to indicate spaces or lines above the staff and B to indicated spaces or lines below the staff.

| Middle - C | A | G | E | B |
| LEDGER LINE ____ | SPACE ____ | LINE ____ | SPACE ____ | LINE ____ |

F	D	C	E	G
LINE _____	LEDGER LINE _____	SPACE _____	LINE _____	LINE _____

B	G	D	F	A
LINE _____	LINE _____	LINE _____	SPACE _____	LEDGER LINE _____

E	D	A	C	B
SPACE _____	SPACE _____	SPACE _____	LEDGER LINE _____	LINE _____

The general rule with notes that have stems is that if there are above or on the middle line of the staff, the stems point downward and are orientated on the left side of the note head. Some exceptions may occur for larger or extensive ascending or descending passages or extended technique markings.

Using the staves provided, practice writing notes with stems up and stems down.

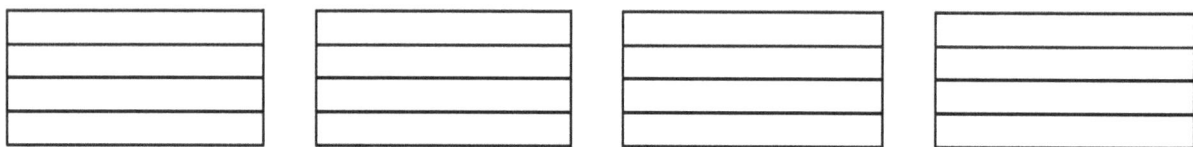

COMMON RESTS

Draw whole rests using the space provided.

Draw half rests using the space provided.

Draw quarter notes using the space provided.

Draw eighth rests using the space provided.

Draw sixteenth rests using the space provided.

COMMON RESTS

Draw the rest indicated by the number of beats.

1 BEAT	**1/2 BEAT**	**2 BEATS**	**4 BEATS**
2 BEATS	**4 BEATS**	**1 BEAT**	**1/2 BEAT**

DOTTED VALUES

DO THE MATH! Draw the notes to complete the equation. Remember that a dot adds one half the value of the note!

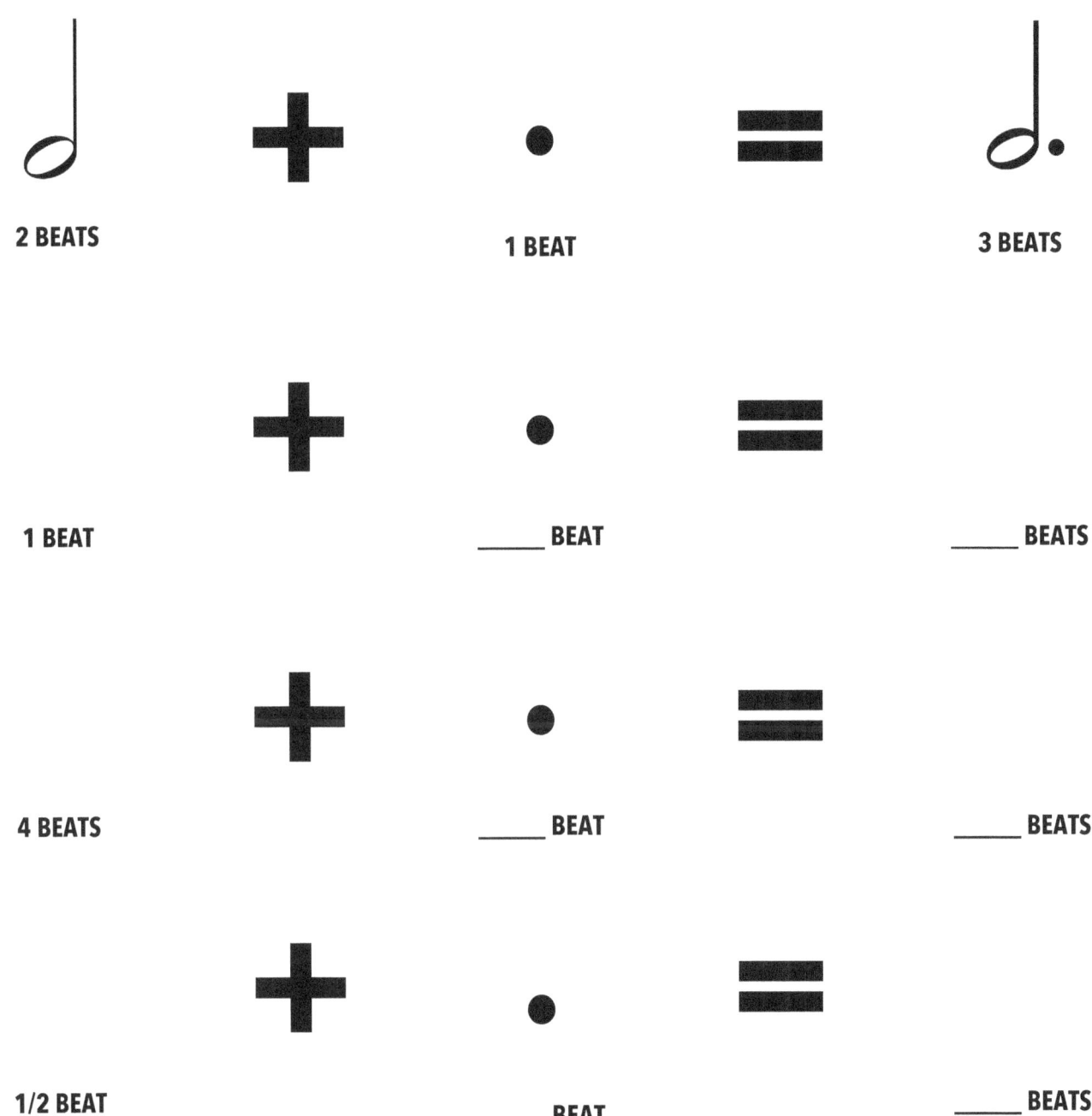

TIME SIGNATURES

Write the correct time signature on the staff for the following excerpts.
Indicate how many beats are in each measure and what type of note gets the beat.

Time Signature: 4/4   Beats per measure: FOUR   Type of note that gets beat: QUARTER NOTE

Time Signature: _____   Beats per measure: _____   Type of note that gets beat: _____

Time Signature: _____   Beats per measure: _____   Type of note that gets beat: _____

Time Signature: _____   Beats per measure: _____   Type of note that gets beat: _____

Time Signature: _____   Beats per measure: _____   Type of note that gets beat: _____

Time Signature: _____   Beats per measure: _____   Type of note that gets beat: _____

Time Signature: _____   Beats per measure: _____   Type of note that gets beat: _____

ACCIDENTALS

Draw a quarter note on the staff for the pitch indicated by the text. Draw a treble clef before you draw the note.

C - Natural	A - Flat	G - Sharp	E - Flat	B - Flat
F - Sharp	A - Natural	C - Sharp	E - Sharp	G - Flat
B - Natural	G - Natural	D - Flat	F - Flat	A - Sharp
E - Sharp	D - Sharp	A - Natural	C - Sharp	B - Sharp

SIMPLE METER

Identify the beat and subdivisions for each meter. Circle the correct classification duple, triple, or quadruple.

Beat: QUARTER NOTE   **Subdivision:** 2 EIGHTH NOTES   **Type:** SIMPLE QUADRUPLE

[4/4 time signature musical example]

Beat: _____   **Subdivision:** _____   **Type:** _____

[3/4 time signature musical example]

Beat: _____   **Subdivision:** _____   **Type:** _____

[2/2 time signature musical example]

Beat: _____   **Subdivision:** _____   **Type:** _____

[2/4 time signature musical example]

Beat: _____   **Subdivision:** _____   **Type:** _____

[4/8 time signature musical example]

Beat: _____   **Subdivision:** _____   **Type:** _____

[2/2 time signature musical example]

Beat: _____   **Subdivision:** _____   **Type:** _____

[3/2 time signature musical example]

COMPOUND METER

Identify the correct time signature. Circle the correct classification duple, triple, or quadruple.

Beat: DOTTED QUARTER NOTE   Subdivision: 3 EIGHTH NOTES   Type: SIMPLE DUPLE

Beat: _____   Subdivision: _____   Type: _____

Beat: _____   Subdivision: _____   Type: _____

Beat: _____   Subdivision: _____   Type: _____

Beat: _____   Subdivision: _____   Type: _____

Beat: _____   Subdivision: _____   Type: _____

Beat: _____   Subdivision: _____   Type: _____

INTERVALS - IDENTIFICATION

Identify the interval.

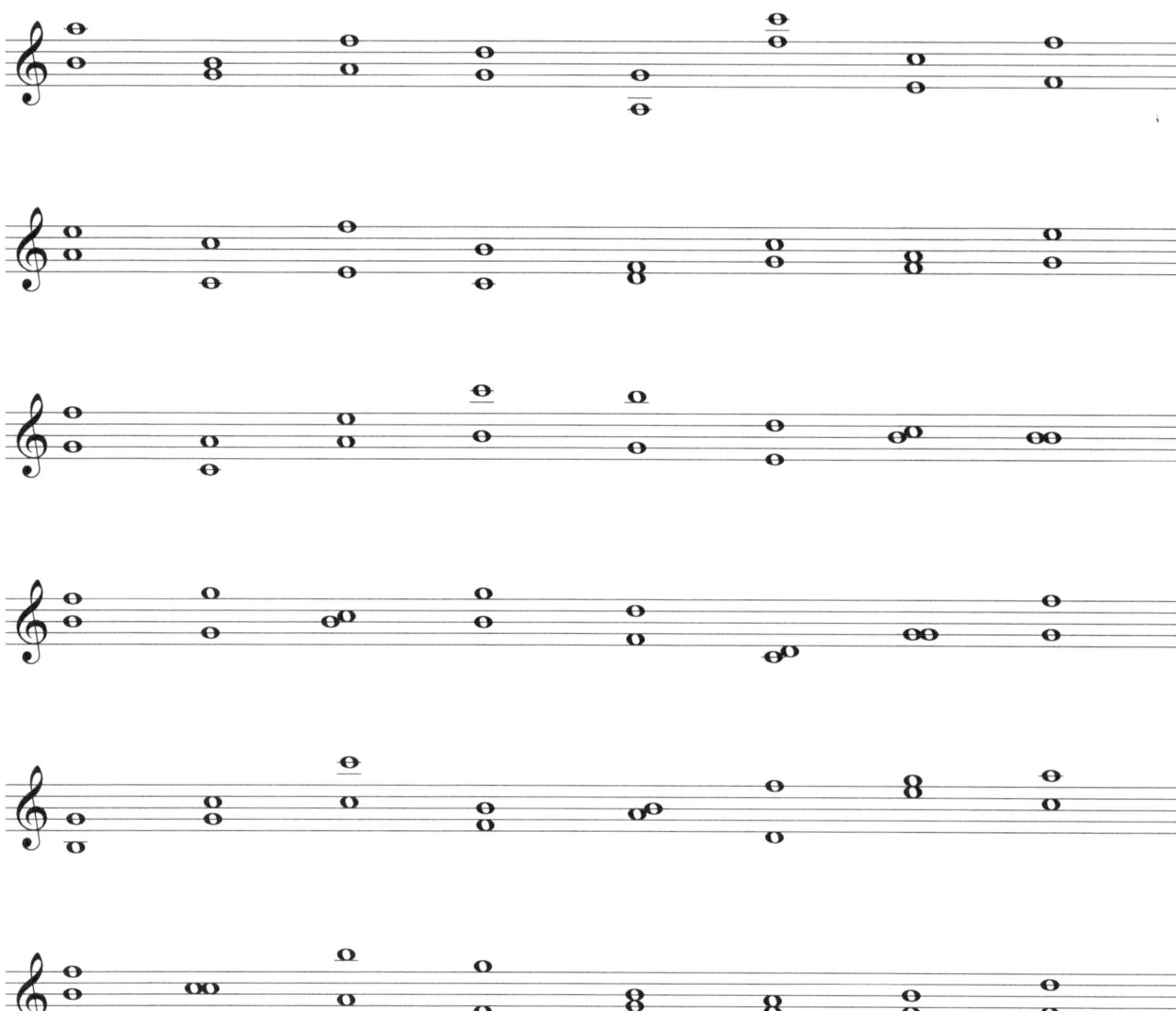

INTERVALS – WRITING INTERVALS

Write the interval above the note using the staves provided. Remember to draw a treble clef before you begin and add ledger lines where necessary.

| THIRD | SECOND | FOURTH | FIFTH | SIXTH |

| FOURTH | OCTAVE | SEVENTH | NINTH | SECOND |

| SIXTH | SEVENTH | OCTAVE | TENTH | FOURTH |

| NINTH | FIFTH | FOURTH | SIXTH | THIRD |

| TENTH | THIRD | OCTAVE | SECOND | FIFTH |

INTERVALS – SPELLING

Complete the patterns.

THIRDS

A	___	E	___	G	B
F	___	___	E	___	___
B	D	___	A	___	___
G	___	___	___	___	C

FIFTHS

F	C	___	D	___	___
E	___	F	___	___	___
B	___	___	G	___	___
G	___	___	___	___	___

INVERTING INTERVALS

Identify the interval, write and label the inversion below the given interval.

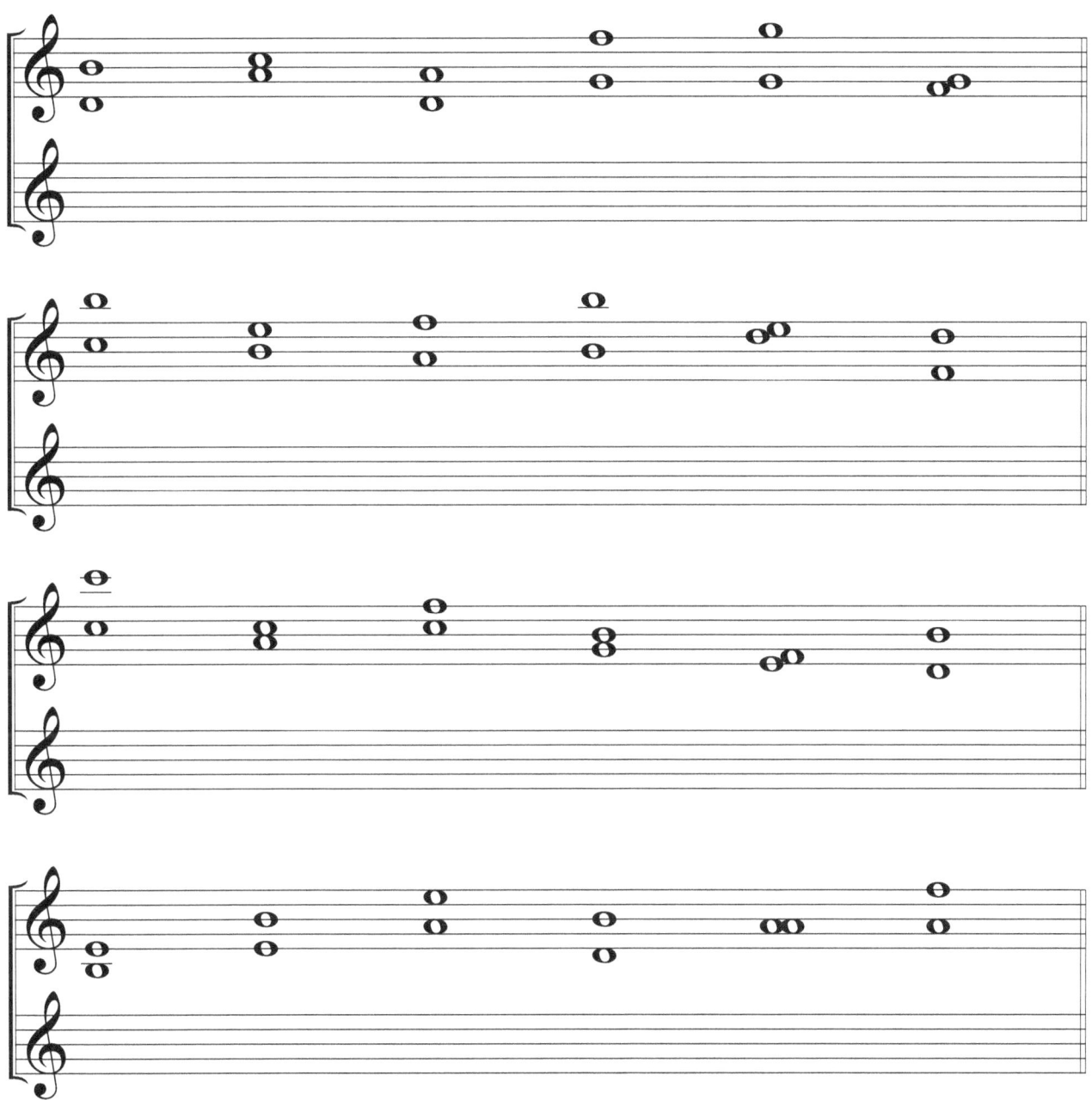

CIRCLE OF FIFTHS

Draw and label your own Circle of Fifths chart. Indicate the number of accidentals natural to each key signature.
A circle has been provided to get you started. You may refer to the chart in the text if you need help.

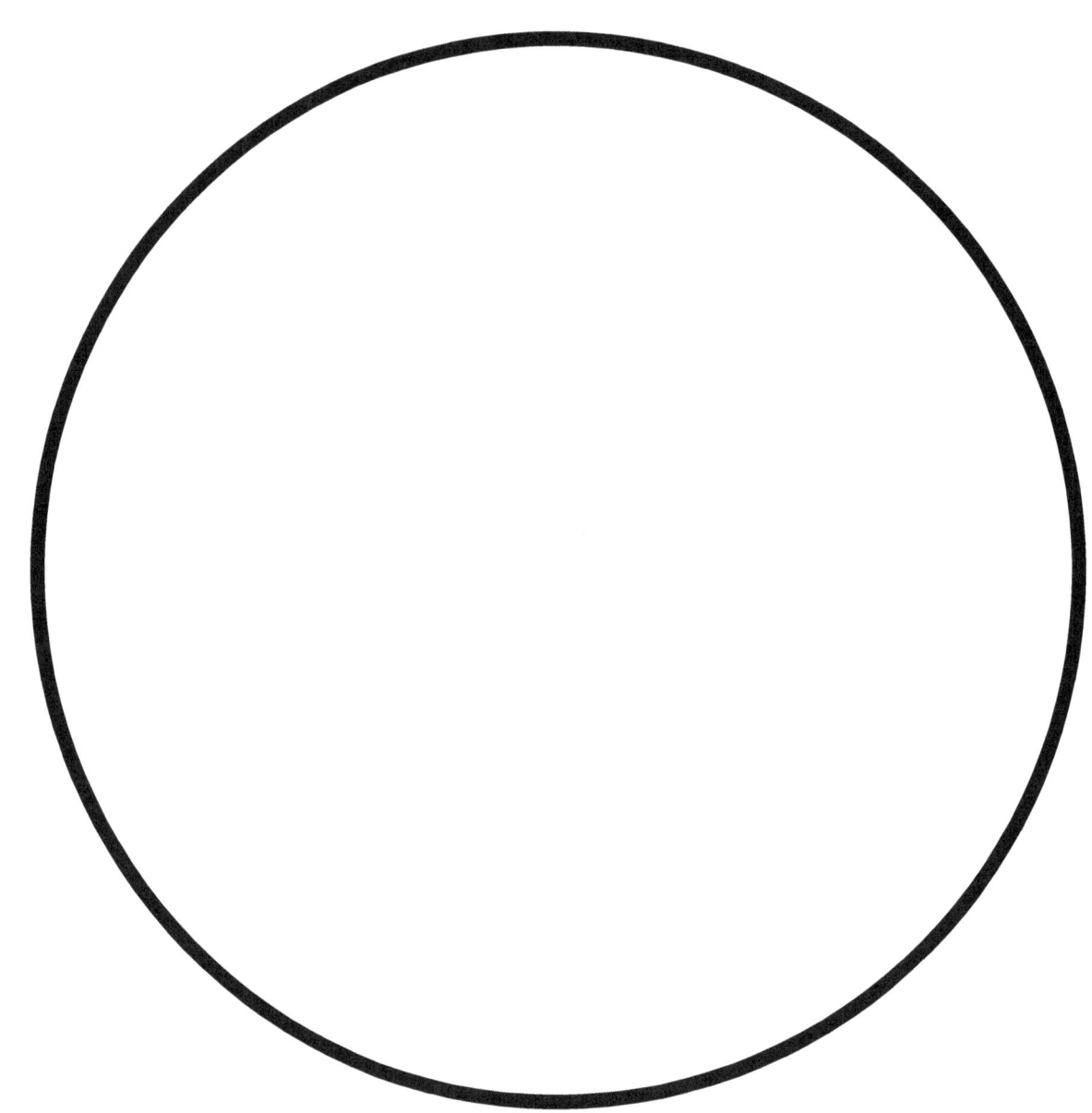

DIATONIC SCALES

Complete the indicated scale, using the pitch provided. Add the accidentals natural to the key signature next to the notes as you draw the scale. You may refer to the charts in the text for assistance.

DIATONIC CHORDS

Using the staves provided write and label the diatonic chords for the following keys:

C Major   a melodic minor   e harmonic minor   F Major   D-flat Major   f natural minor

ADDITIONAL MANUSCRIPT FOR NOTES

Use the following pages for notation of your own musical ideas, or as scratch paper for figuring out musical ideas discussed in the text and writing sections of this book. You may also, use this area to try transposing phrases within the book into other keys.

PLAYING EXERCISES

RHYTHM STUDIES

Simple Meter Exercises

Compound Meter Exercises

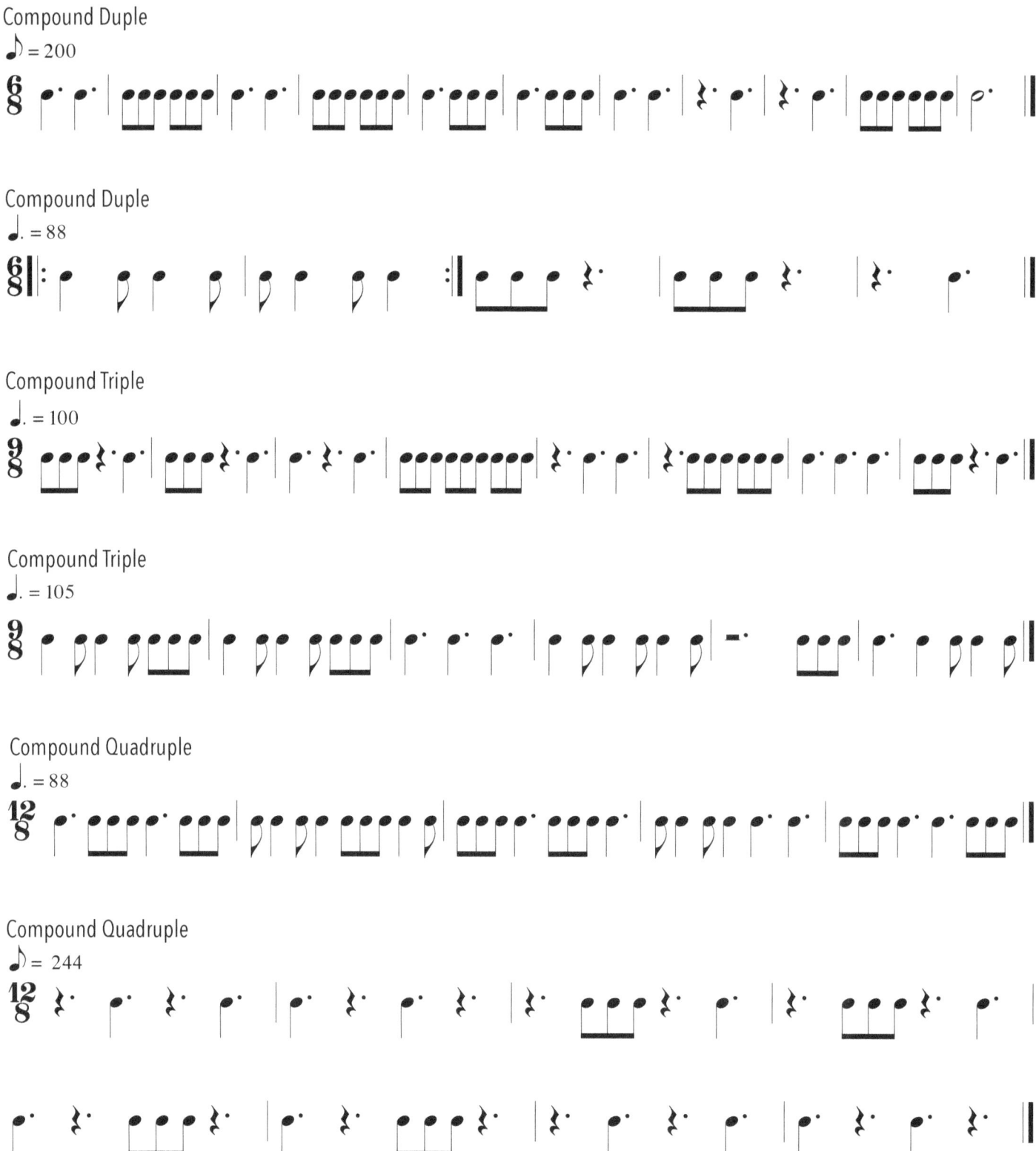

General Practice Rhythm Exercises

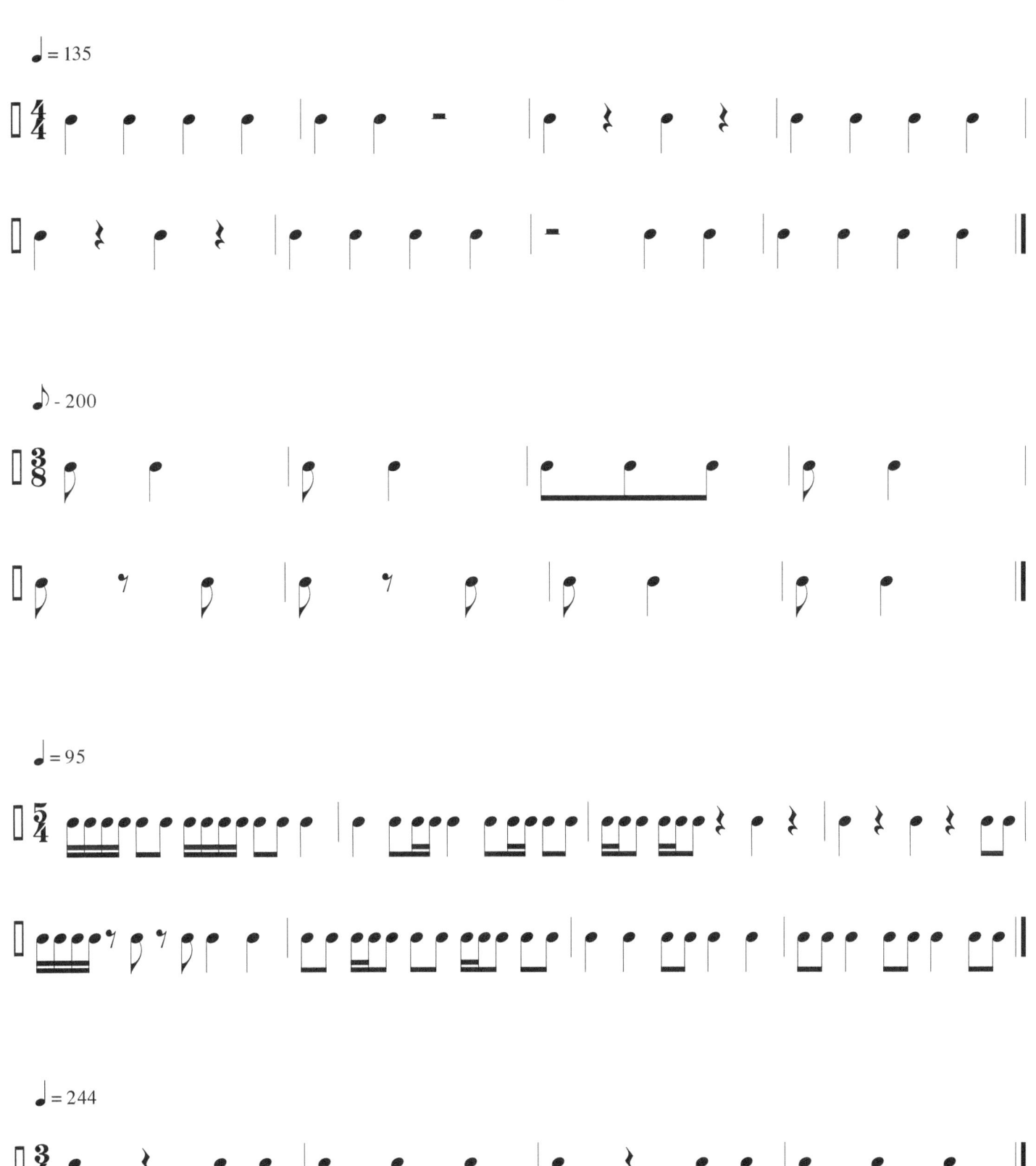

General Practice Rhythm Exercises

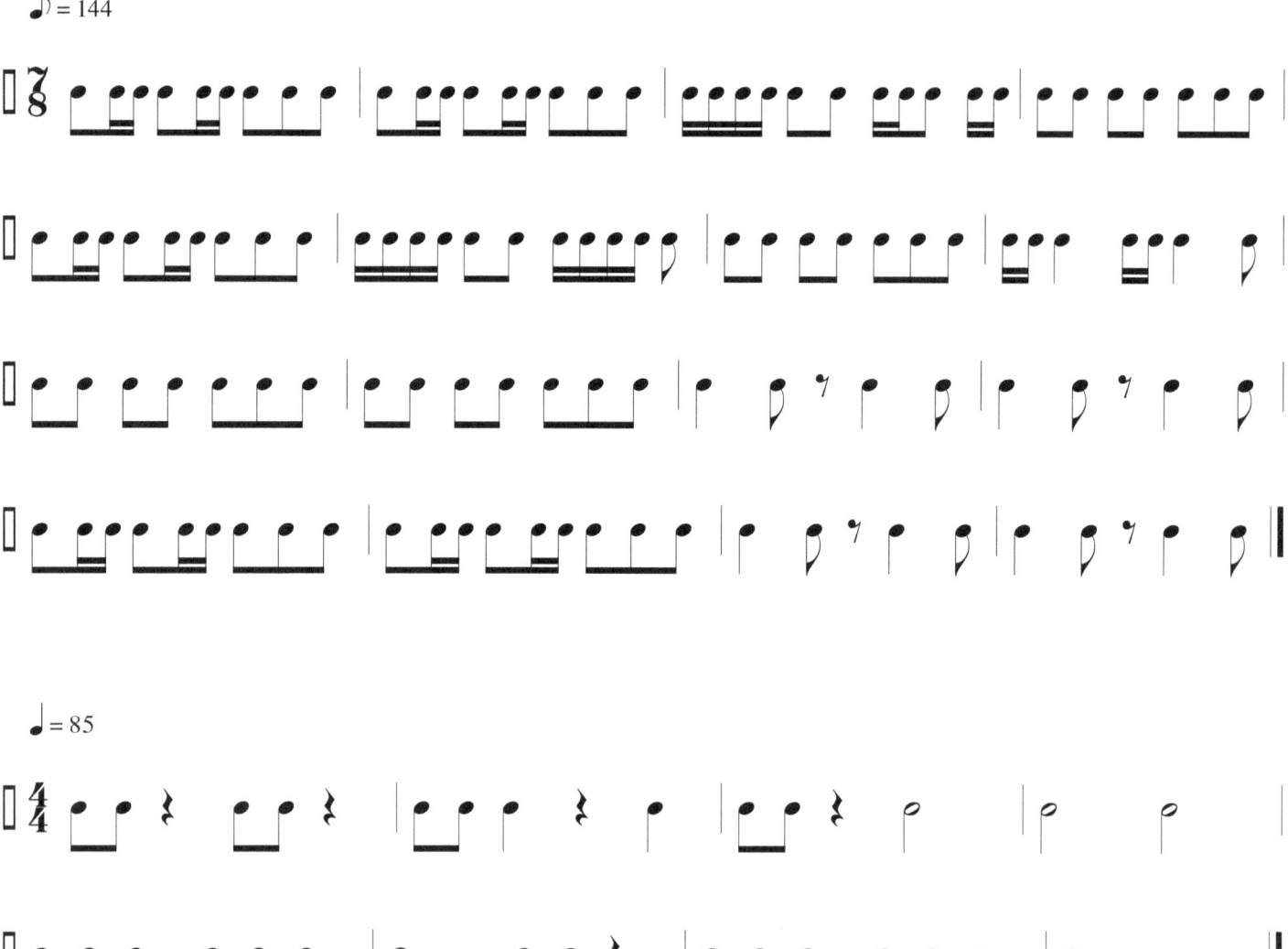

General Practice Rhythm Exercises

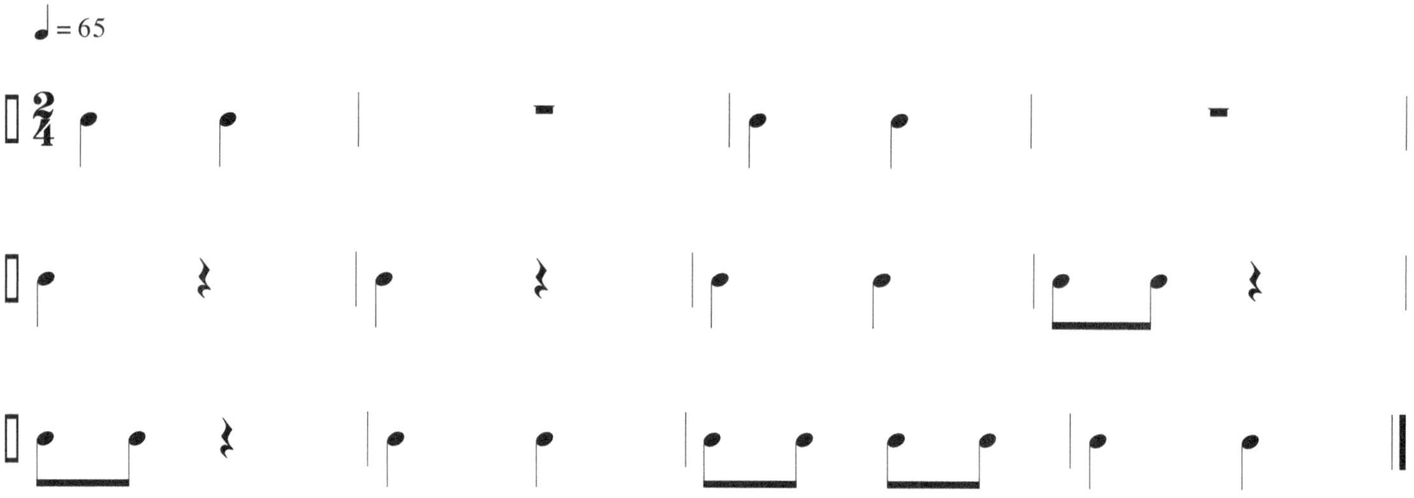

General Practice Rhythm Exercises

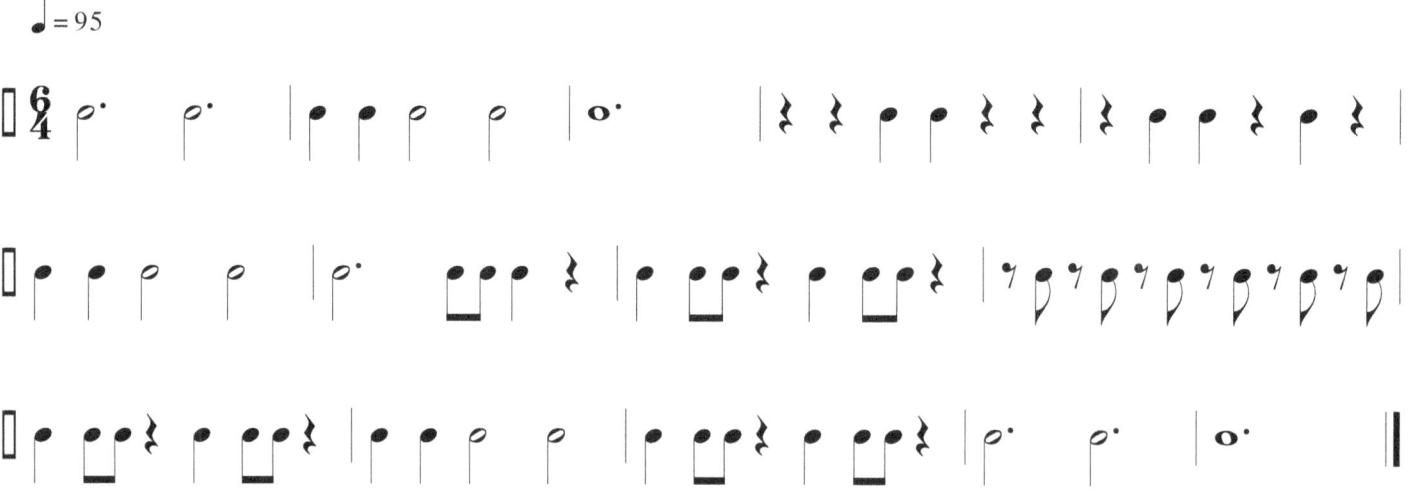

General Practice Rhythm Exercises

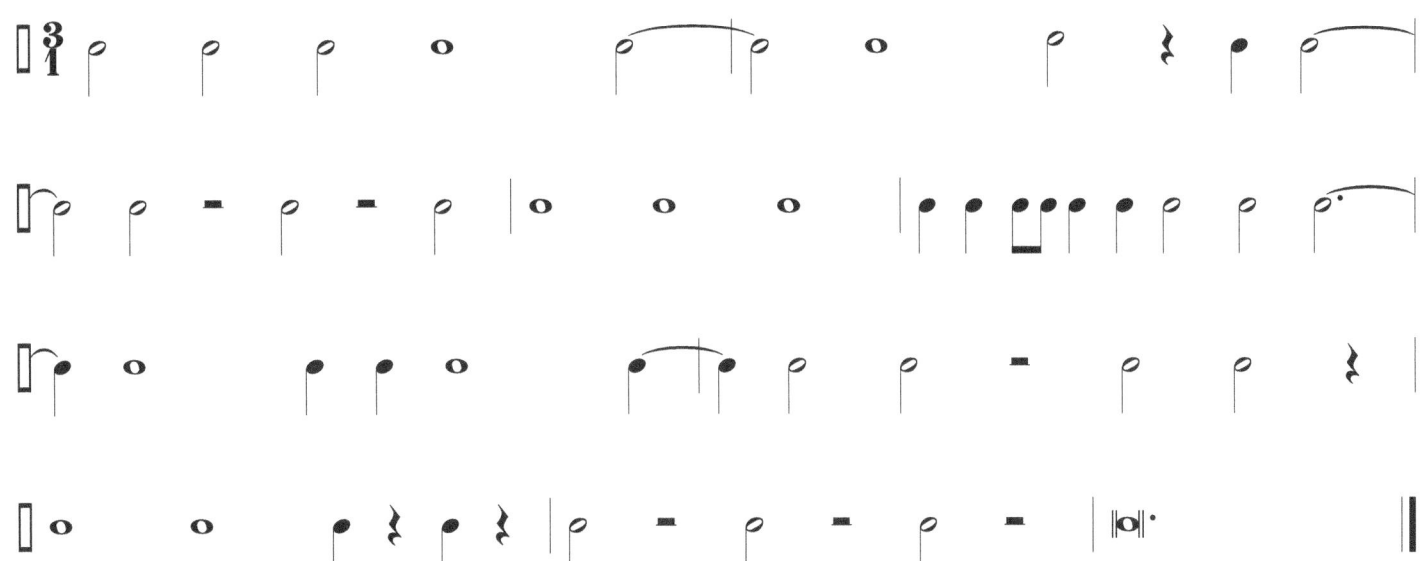

INTERVALS

Interval Studies

Unison - Harmonic

Unison - Melodic

Second - Harmonic

Second - Melodic

Third - Harmonic

Third - Melodic

Interval Studies

Fourth - Harmonic

Fourth - Melodic

Fifth - Harmonic

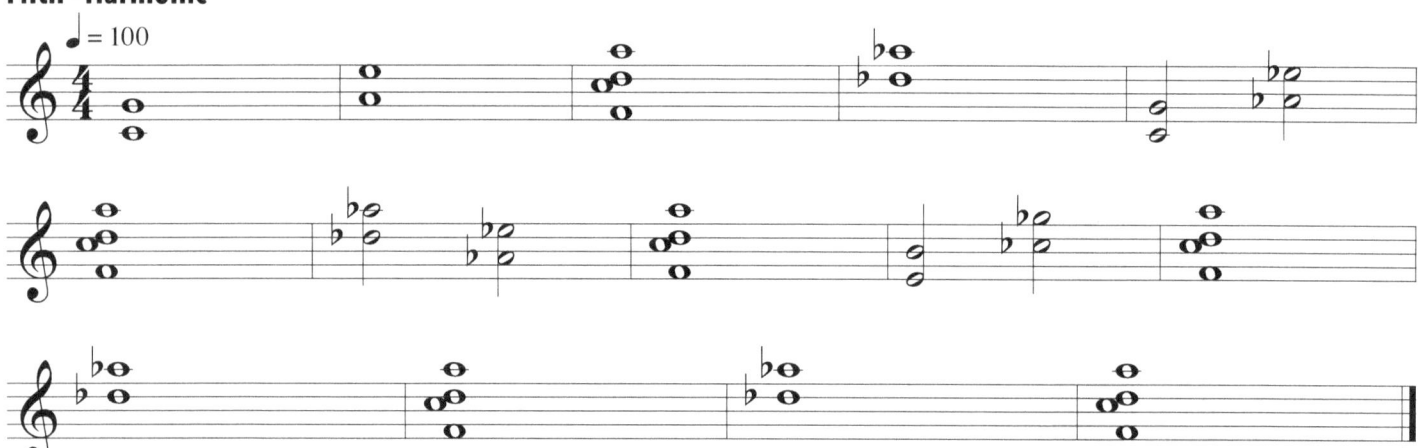

Interval Studies

Fifth - Melodic

Sixth - Harmonic

Sixth - Harmonic

Seventh - Harmonic

Interval Studies

Seventh - Melodic

Octave - Harmonic

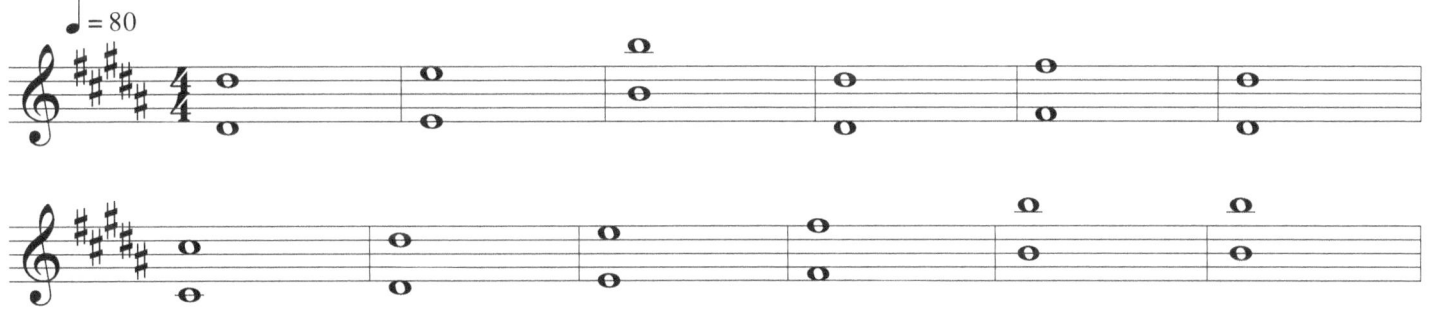

Octave - Melodic

SCALES

White Key Major Pentachord Scales

C Major   C D E F G   Right Hand: 1 2 3 4 5
                                Left Hand: 5 4 3 2 1

G Major   G A B C D   Right Hand: 1 2 3 4 5
                                Left Hand: 5 4 3 2 1

D Major   D E F♯ G A   Right Hand: 1 2 3 4 5
                                Left Hand: 5 4 3 2 1

A Major   A B C♯ D E   Right Hand: 1 2 3 4 5
                                Left Hand: 5 4 3 2 1

E Major   E F♯ G♯ A B   Right Hand: 1 2 3 4 5
                                Left Hand: 5 4 3 2 1

B Major   B C♯ D♯ E F♯   Right Hand: 1 2 3 4 5
                                Left Hand: 5 4 3 2 1

F Major   F G A B♭ C   Right Hand: 1 2 3 4 5
                                Left Hand: 5 4 3 2 1

White Key Minor Pentachord Scales

a minor   A B C D E   Right Hand: 1 2 3 4 5
                                       Left Hand: 5 4 3 2 1

e minor   E F♯ G A B   Right Hand: 1 2 3 4 5
                                       Left Hand: 5 4 3 2 1

b minor   B C♯ D E F♯   Right Hand: 1 2 3 4 5
                                       Left Hand: 5 4 3 2 1

f minor   F G A♭ B♭ C   Right Hand: 1 2 3 4 5
                                       Left Hand: 5 4 3 2 1

c minor   C D E♭ F G   Right Hand: 1 2 3 4 5
                                       Left Hand: 5 4 3 2 1

g minor   G A B♭ C D   Right Hand: 1 2 3 4 5
                                       Left Hand: 5 4 3 2 1

d minor   D E F G A   Right Hand: 1 2 3 4 5
                                       Left Hand: 5 4 3 2 1

Black Key Major Pentachord Scales

B♭ Major B♭ C D E♭ F Right Hand: 2 1 2 3 4
Left Hand: 5 4 3 2 1

E♭ Major E♭ F G A♭ B♭ Right Hand: 2 1 2 3 4
Left Hand: 5 4 3 2 1

A♭ Major A♭ B♭ C D♭ E♭ Right Hand: 2 3 1 2 3
Left Hand: 5 4 3 2 1

D♭ Major D♭ E♭ F G♭ A♭
C♯ Major C♯ D♯ E♯ F♯ G♯ Right Hand: 2 3 1 2 3
Left Hand: 5 4 3 2 1

G♭ Major G♭ A♭ B♭ C♭ D♭
F♯ Major F♯ G♯ A♯ B C♯ Right Hand: 2 3 4 1 2
Left Hand: 5 4 3 2 1

Black Key Minor Pentachord Scales

f♯ minor F♯ G♯ A B C♯
Right Hand: 2 3 1 2 3
Left Hand: 5 4 3 2 1

c♯ minor C♯ D♯ E F♯ G♯
Right Hand: 2 3 1 2 3
Left Hand: 5 4 3 2 1

a♭ minor A♭ B♭ C♭ D♭ E♭
Right Hand: 2 3 1 2 3
g♯ minor G♯ A♯ B C♯ D♯
Left Hand: 5 4 3 2 1

e♭ minor E♭ F G♭ A♭ B♭
Right Hand: 2 1 2 3 4
d♯ minor D♯ E♯ F♯ G♯ A♯
Left Hand: 5 4 3 2 1

b♭ minor B♭ C D♭ E♭ F
Right Hand: 2 1 2 3 4
a♯ minor A♯ B♯ C♯ D♯ E♯
Left Hand: 5 4 3 2 1

Full Scales

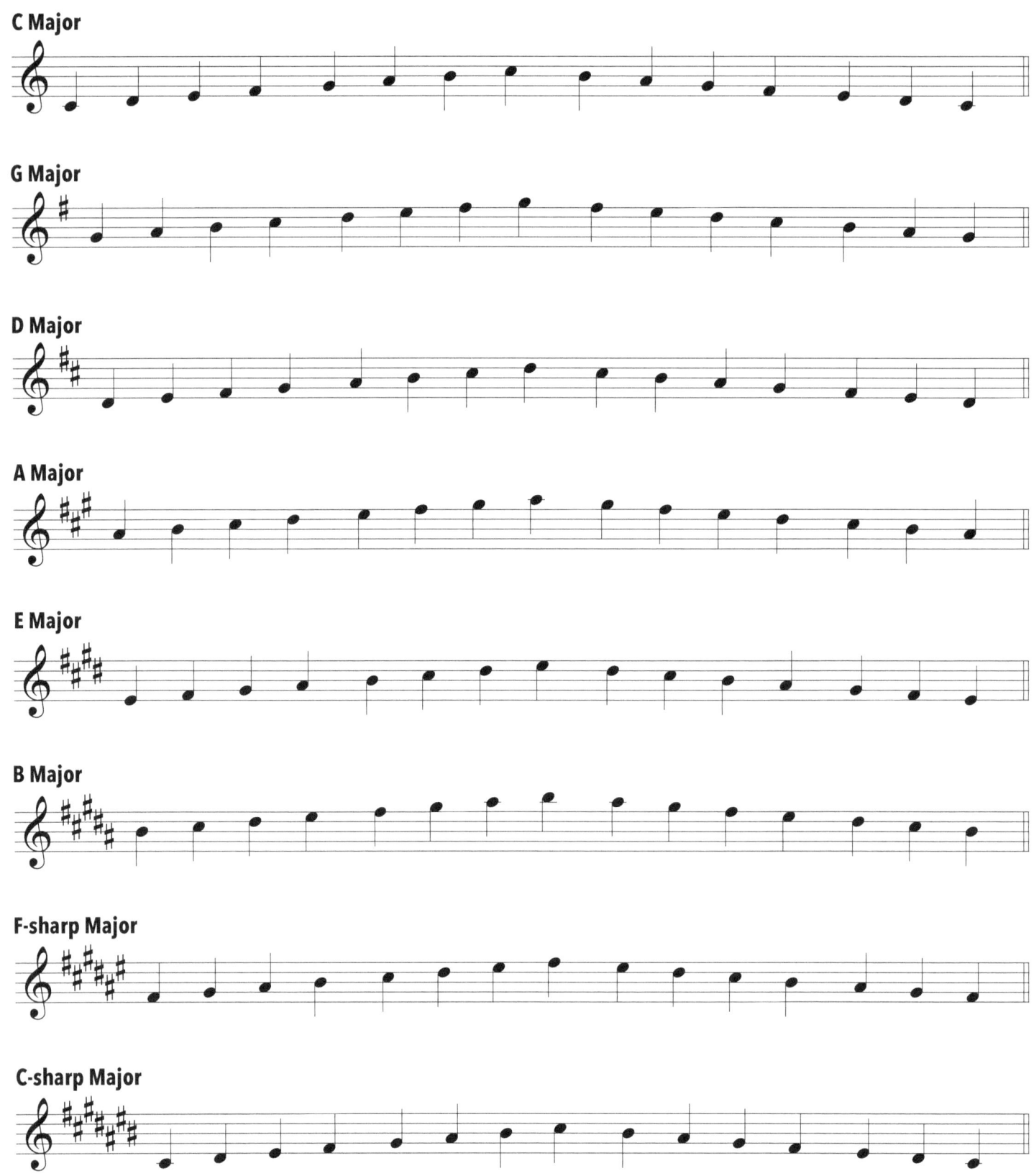

Full Scales

F Major

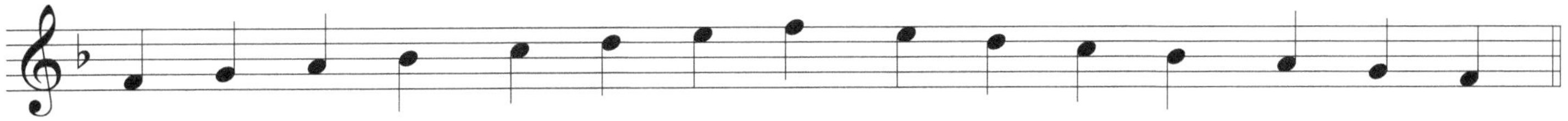

B-flat Major

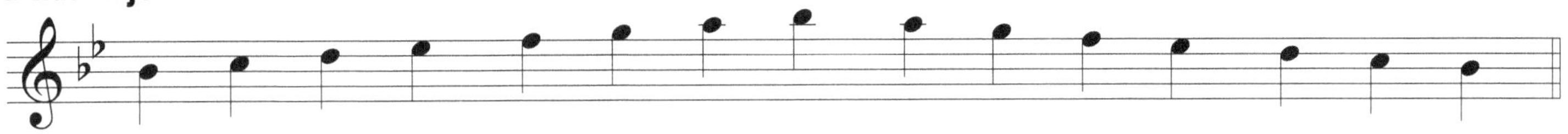

E-flat Major

A-flat Major

D-flat Major

G-flat Major

a minor

e minor

b minor

Full Scales

f-sharp minor

c-sharp minor

g-sharp minor

d-sharp minor

a-sharp minor

d minor

g minor

c minor

f minor

Full Scales

b-flat minor

e-flat minor

PATTERNS

Patterns

These patterns may be practiced at any speed, as long as the student maintains physical control and plays without tension. The patterns may also be transposed in to a variety of keys and modes, for practice of transposition at sight.

Patterns

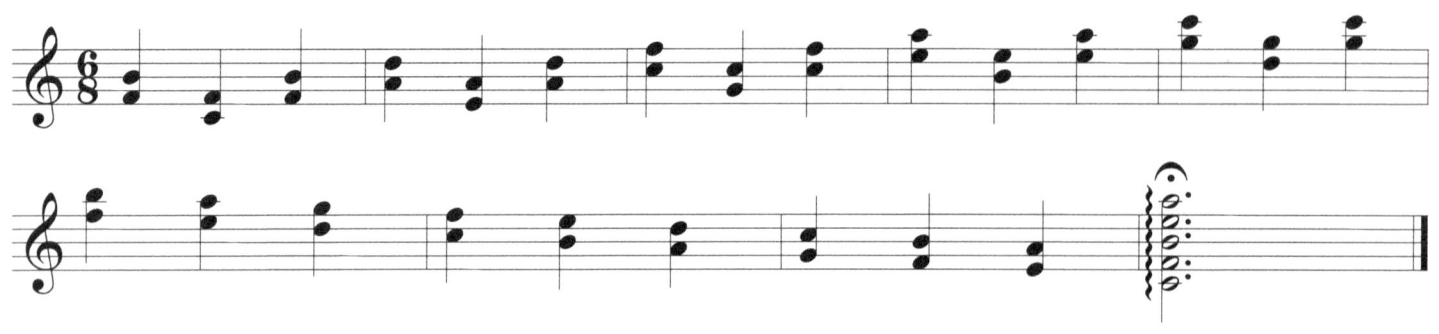

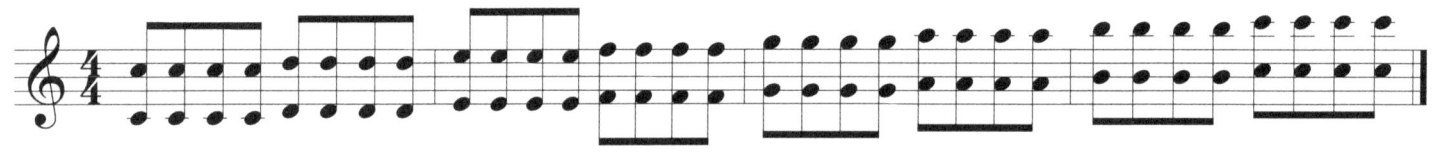
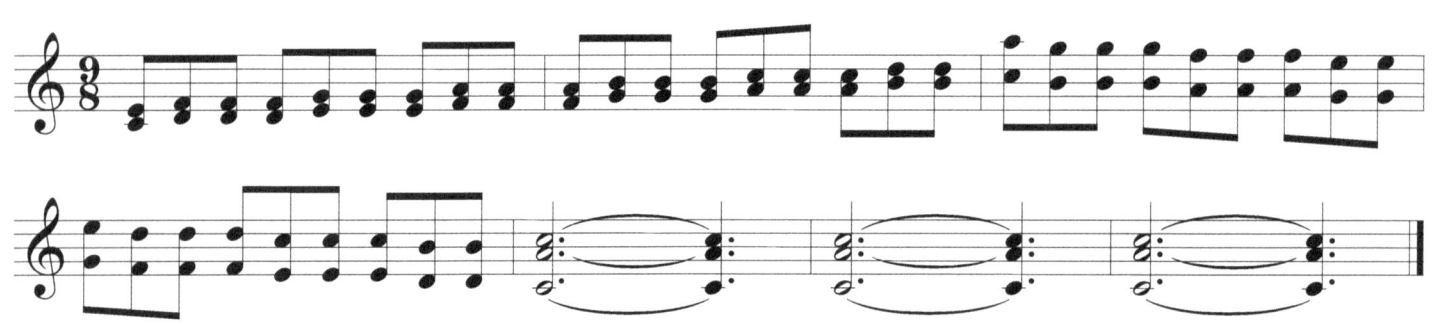

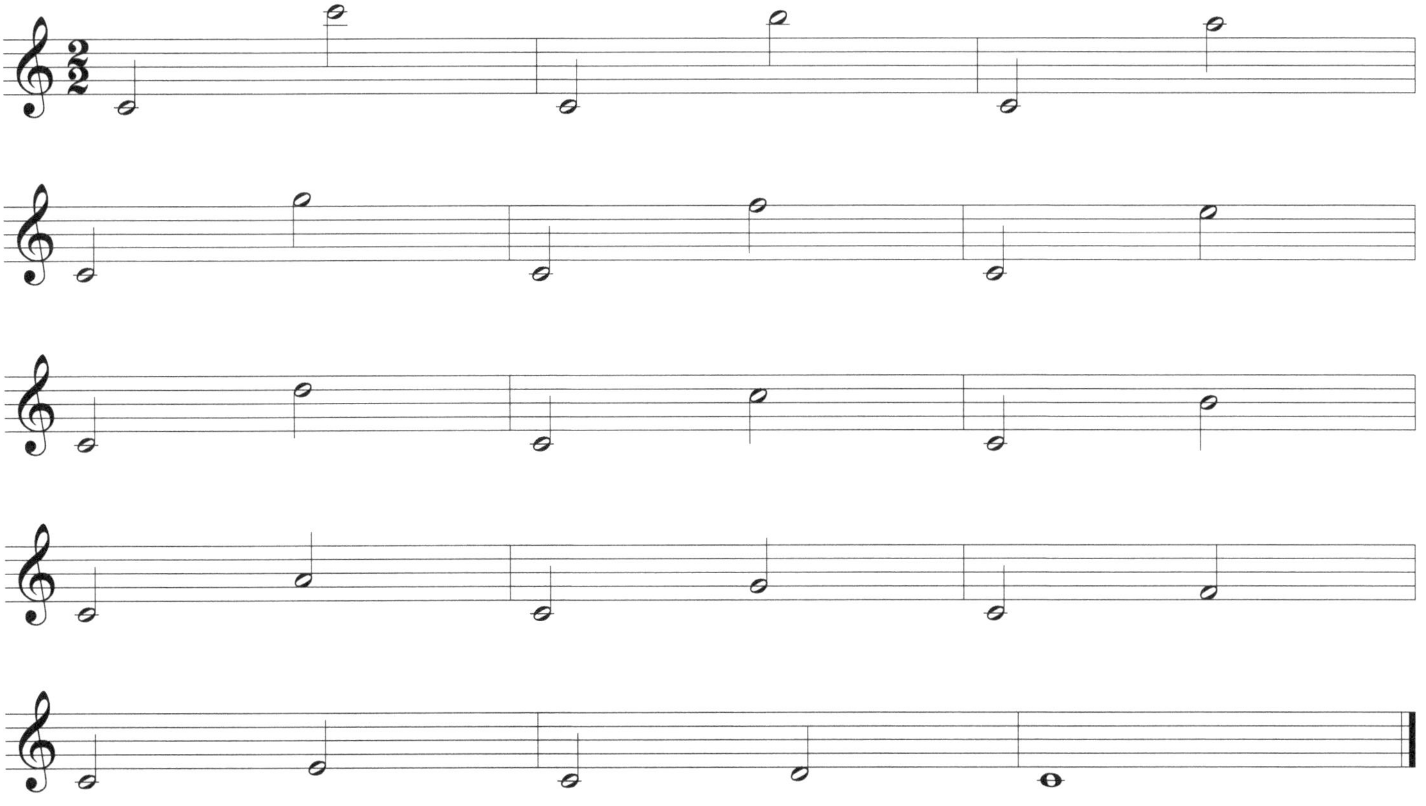

Patterns

SOLO WORKS

Just Getting Started

A Little Familiar

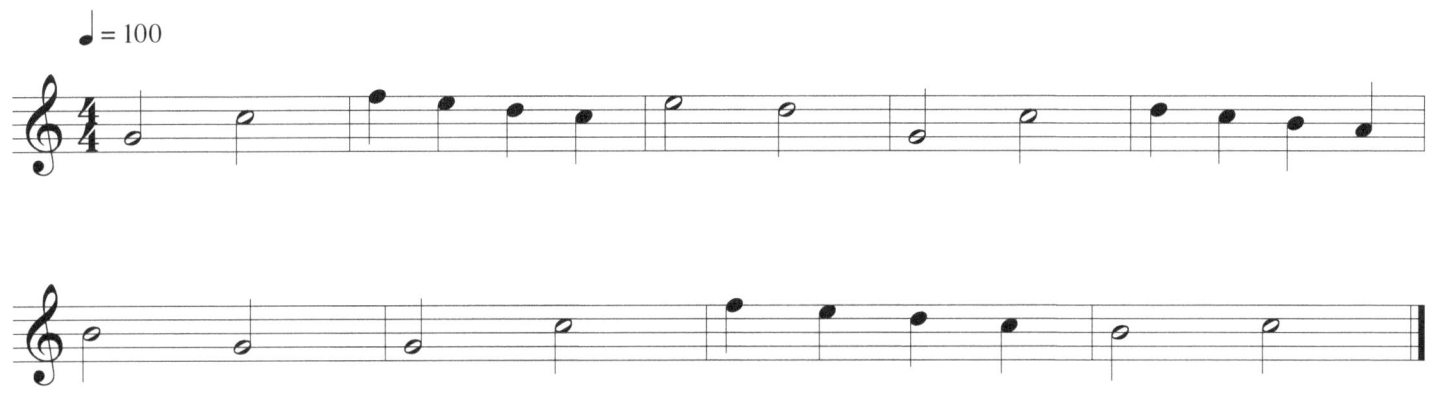

Ding! Ding!

I Don't Want To...

Baby Powder

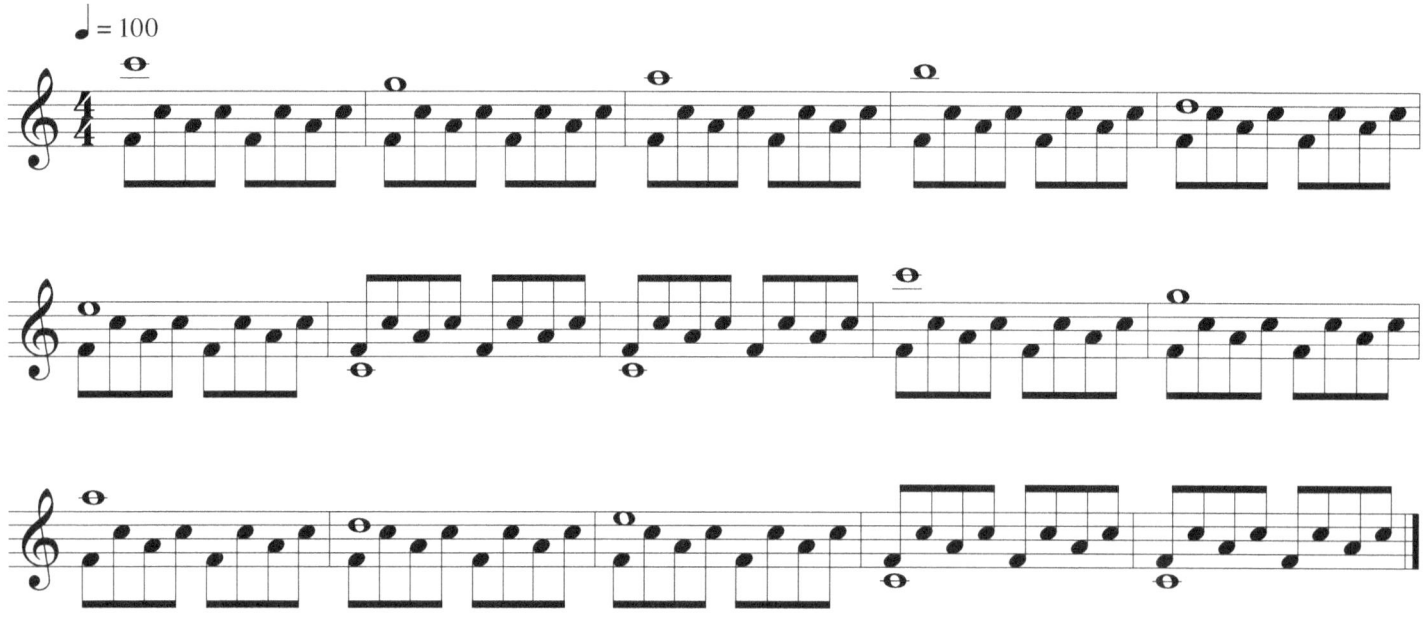

Fragile Insides

Tick! Tick! Ding!

The Ice's Illusion

Fulfillment is a constant...

The Wizards's Petals

The Rising Flowers

Saltarello

Anonymous

Pavana II

Luis de Milan
Arr. Elizabeth A. Baker

Pavana II

Minuet

J.S. Bach

Etude No. 8
Op. 60, No. 8

M. Carcassi
Arr. Elizabeth A. Baker

Calm & Jitters

Meditative Confusion ♩ = 100

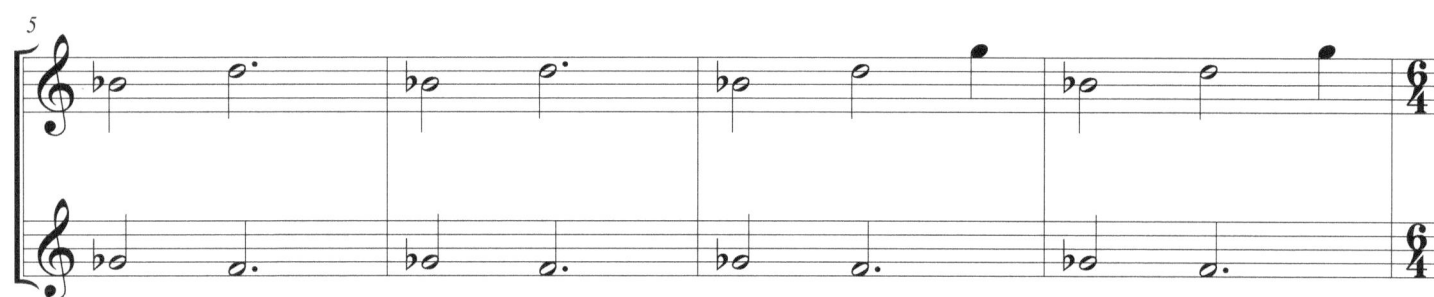

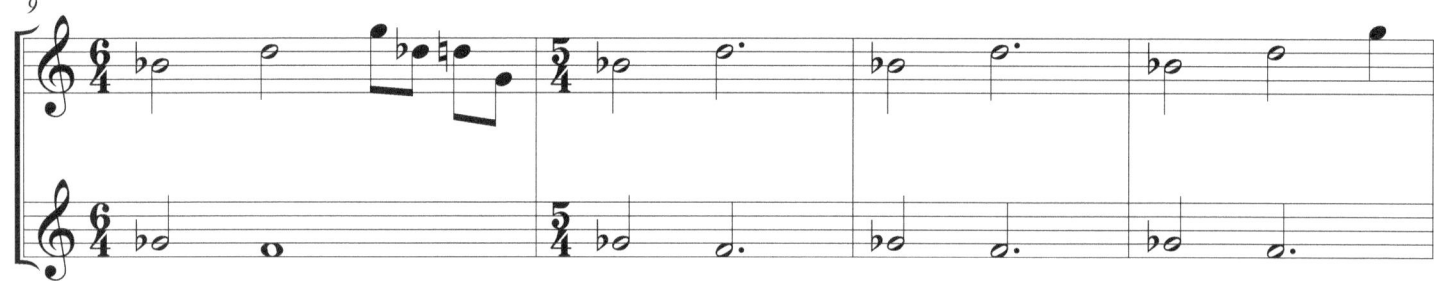

Emerging Chaos ♩ = 148

Calm & Jitters

Calm & Jitters

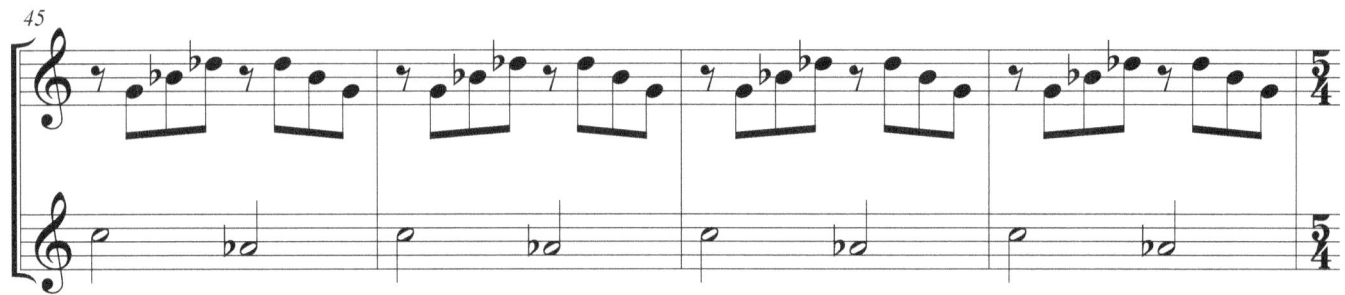

Meditative Confusion ♩ = 100

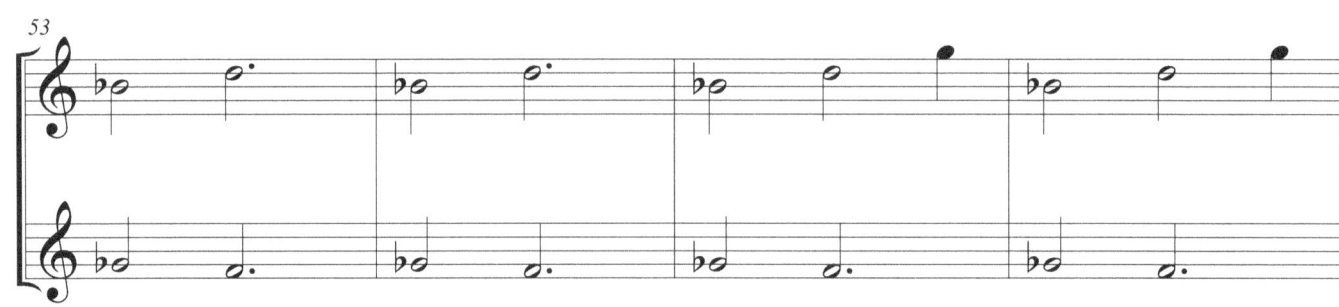

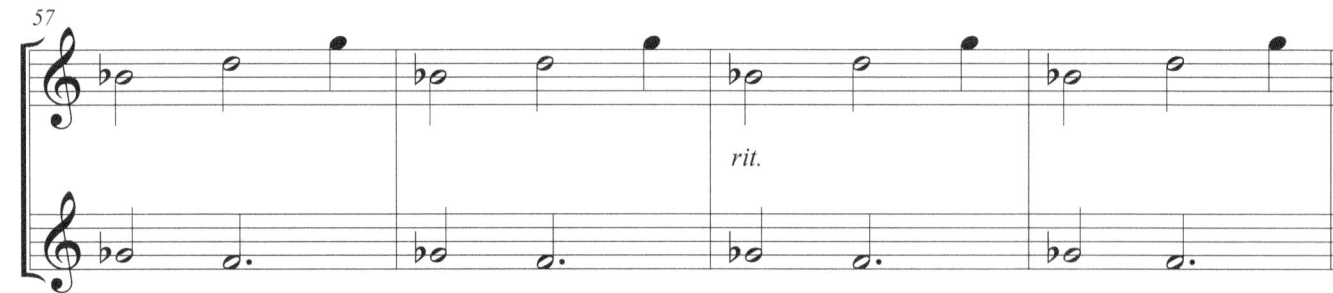

Andante

Ferdinando Carulli
Arr. Elizabeth A. Baker

D.C. al Fine

An Icy Valentine

IMPROVISATION

Harmonic Improvisation

Improvise over the given chord progression.

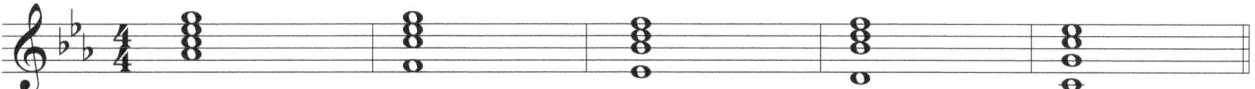

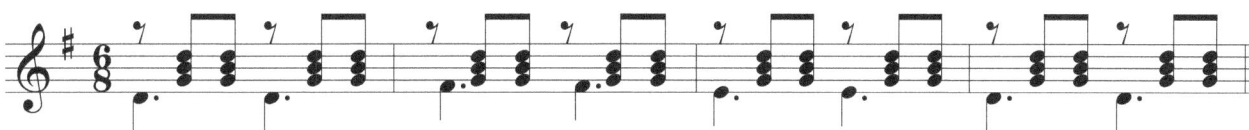

Electronic accompaniment is available via *Soundcloud* for this section.
Use your ear to figure out the notes, which harmonize best with the electronic accompaniment.

Something Like Love

https://soundcloud.com/toyager/something-like-love

5:00

Nostalgic Cinema

https://soundcloud.com/toyager/nostalgic-cinema

2:30

Someone Exactly Like You

https://soundcloud.com/toyager/someone-exactly-like-you

3:00

Linear Improvisation
Use the provided cells as a starting point for improvisation.
(5-8 minutes each improvisation)

Text Improvisation

Use any of the following words and phrases in pairs or groups of three as the inspiration for a new improvisation. (3-5 minutes per improvisation)

...never stops	gentle	mischievous	shine
armor	graceful	missing	sickness
blind	happenstance	My ideal...	somber
calm	hard	My lover is...	Something on the...
continuous	harmonious	new	sparse
Did you really...	heartfelt	ocean	strong
discord	heroic	oil	struggle
disdain	homeland	old	tears
disjointed	horizon	painting	thin veneer
distant lands	I couldn't allow myself to...	peaceful	tomorrow
drama	I saw you...	philosophy	travel
dreams	life	pompous	trouble
earth	love	possibility	water
For you I would...	mask	powerful	willing
forever	mask	problem	without
frustration		royal	yesterday

Other Prompts for Structured Improvisation

Using the following parameters to improvise.

(3-5 minutes per improvisation)

Chains of sevenths (intervals)

Sparse textures to dense textures

Undulating pulsing of loud and soft

Student's choice

Soft and dense textures

Loud and sparse textures

Interconnected Circles

Angular textures

Consider the following graphics for separate improvisation:

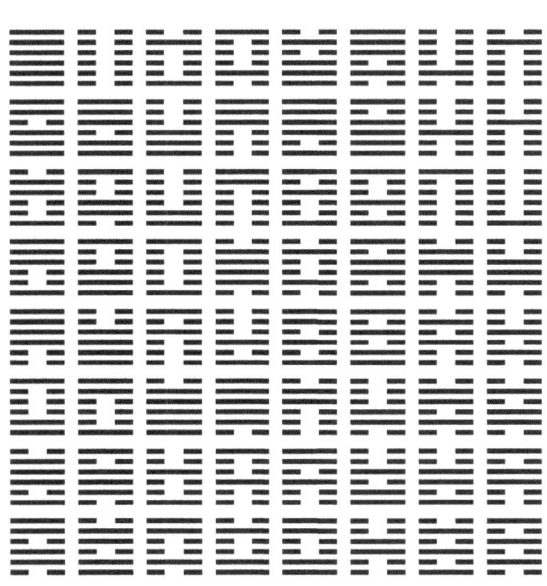

PRACTICE PLANNER

Practice Planner

Date: _____ / _____ / _____

Technical Studies	Repertoire	Improvisation/Free Study
Scales _____ _____ _____ **Chords** _____ _____ _____ **Other** _____ _____ _____	_____ _____ _____ _____ _____ _____ _____ _____ _____ _____ _____ _____	_____ _____ _____ _____ _____ _____ _____ _____ _____ _____ _____ _____
Time Spent: _____	Time Spent: _____	Time Spent: _____

Notes:

_____
_____
_____
_____
_____

Practice Planner

Date: _____ / _____ / _____

Technical Studies	Repertoire	Improvisation/Free Study
Scales _____ _____ _____ **Chords** _____ _____ _____ **Other** _____ _____ _____ _____	_____ _____ _____ _____ _____ _____ _____ _____ _____ _____ _____ _____ _____	_____ _____ _____ _____ _____ _____ _____ _____ _____ _____ _____ _____ _____
Time Spent: _____	Time Spent: _____	Time Spent: _____

Notes:

_____

_____

_____

_____

_____

Practice Planner

Date: _____ / _____ / _____

Technical Studies	Repertoire	Improvisation/Free Study
Scales		
Chords		
Other		
Time Spent: _____	Time Spent: _____	Time Spent: _____

Notes:

_____

_____

_____

_____

_____

Practice Planner

Date: _____ / _____ / _____

Technical Studies	Repertoire	Improvisation/Free Study
Scales _____ _____ _____ **Chords** _____ _____ _____ **Other** _____ _____ _____ _____	_____ _____ _____ _____ _____ _____ _____ _____ _____ _____ _____ _____ _____ _____	_____ _____ _____ _____ _____ _____ _____ _____ _____ _____ _____ _____ _____ _____
Time Spent: _____	Time Spent: _____	Time Spent: _____

Notes:

_____
_____
_____
_____
_____

Practice Planner

Date: _____ / _____ / _____

Technical Studies	Repertoire	Improvisation/Free Study
Scales _____ _____ _____ **Chords** _____ _____ _____ **Other** _____ _____ _____	_____ _____ _____ _____ _____ _____ _____ _____ _____ _____ _____ _____	_____ _____ _____ _____ _____ _____ _____ _____ _____ _____ _____ _____
Time Spent: _____	Time Spent: _____	Time Spent: _____

Notes:

_____

_____

_____

_____

_____

Practice Planner

Date: _____ / _____ / _____

Technical Studies	Repertoire	Improvisation/Free Study
Scales _____ _____ _____ **Chords** _____ _____ _____ **Other** _____ _____ _____ _____	_____ _____ _____ _____ _____ _____ _____ _____ _____ _____ _____ _____ _____	_____ _____ _____ _____ _____ _____ _____ _____ _____ _____ _____ _____ _____
Time Spent: _____	Time Spent: _____	Time Spent: _____

Notes:

_____
_____
_____
_____
_____
_____

Bibliography

Bamberger, W.C. "Chrysalis and Absence: Some Notes on Margaret Leng Tan (Part 2)." 2007 йил August. Perfect Sound Forever. 2016 йил 1-March <http://www.furious.com/perfect/lengtan2.html>.

–. "Chrysalis and Absence: Some Notes on Margret Leng Tan (Part 1)." 2007 йил August. Perfect Sound Forever. 2016 йил 1-March <http://www.furious.com/perfect/lengtan.html>.

British Broadcasting Corporation. "Cut And Splice 2005: Mauricio Kagel." 2005. BBC Radio. 2016 йил 1-March <http://www.bbc.co.uk/radio3/cutandsplice/kagel.shtml>.

Brookes, Stephen. "Margaret Leng Tan reigns over a toy piano renaissance." 2014 йил 3-October. The Washington Post. 2016 йил 1-March <https://www.washingtonpost.com/entertainment/music/margaret-leng-tan-reigns-over-a-toy-piano-renaissance/2014/10/03/756396c2-45bb-11e4-9a15-137aa0153527_story.html>.

Chen, Phyllis. Phyllis Chen. 2016 йил March <http://www.phyllischen.net/>.

Crumb, George. Composer George Crumb: A Conversation with Bruce Duffie Bruce Duffie. 1988 йил 27-August.
–. George Crumb Biography. 2016 йил 1-March <http://www.georgecrumb.net/>.

Dunn, Arlene and Larry Dunn. "5 questions to Phyllis Chen (Director, UnCaged Toy Piano Festival)." 2013 йил 6-December. I Care If You Listen. 2016 йил 1-March <http://www.icareifyoulisten.com/2013/12/5-questions-to-phyllis-chen-director-uncaged-toy-piano-festival/>.

Ettenauer, Isabel. "A Short Introduction to the Music for Toy Piano by Karlheinz Essl." Fowl Feathered Review 4 (2013): 74-81.
–. Isabel Ettenauer. 2016 йил 1-March <http://www.isabelettenauer.com/>.

Experimental Music Catalogue. "Who are the PTO? And what is an Orangery?" 1969. Experimental Music Catalogue. 2016 йил 11-February <http://www.experimentalmusic.co.uk/emc/About_the_PTO.html>.

Goodwin, Jeremy. "The Sound Of (New) Music." 2014 йил 1-August. New England Public Radio. 2016 йил 1-March <http://nepr.net/news/2014/08/01/the-sound-of-new-music/>.

Harvard University Press Reference Library. The Harvard Dictionary of Music. Ed. Don Michael Randel. Fourth Edition. Cambridge: The Belknap Press of Harvard University Press, 2003.

Hoffer, Charles R. The Understanding of Music. Third Edition. Belmont: Wadsworth Publishing Company, Inc., 1976.

Kagel, Mauricio. Interview with Mauricio Kagel Anthony Coleman. Cologne: BOMB Magazine, 2003 йил May.

Kagel, Pamela. Mauricio Kagel Biography. 2016 йил March <http://www.mauricio-kagel.com/gb/biografy.html>.

Pestova, Xenia. Xenia Pestova Biography. 2015 йил June. 2016 йил 1-March <http://www.xeniapestova.com/bio.html>.

Piper Clendinning, Jane and Elizabeth West Marvin. The Musicican's Guide to Theory and Analysis. First Edition. New York City: W.W. Norton & Company, Inc., 2005.

Red Poppy Music, LTD. "Biography." 2016. Juilia Wolfe Music. 2016 йил 1-March <http://juliawolfemusic.com/about/bio>.

Schoenberg, Arnold. Theory of Harmony. Trans. Roy E. Carter. 100th Anniversary Edition. University of California, 1911.

Schoenhut Piano Company. History. 2016 йил 1-March <http://www.toypiano.com/about_history.asp>.

Tan, Margret Leng. Margret Leng Tan. 2015. 2016 йил 1-March <http://margaretlengtan.com/pages/about.html>.

Whiteside, Abby. Indispensables of Piano Playing. Second Edition. New York City: Charles Scribner's Sons, 1955.

Special Thanks To:

Yvonne P. Small Baker my beautiful wonderful mother, who continues to support my love of music, and life as a musician.

Willie M. Baker my devoted father, who always pushes me to do my best.

Fofi Panagiotouros my loving sister, who embodies a genuine care and interest in helping me achieve my dreams; for all of her hard work and dedication to this project.

Schoenhut Piano Company for all their support and commitment to creating quality toy pianos.

Dr. Karlheinz Essl and Tristan Perich for graciously allotting time out of their busy schedules to allow me to interview them for the composer profile section of the book.

Susan Dickson-Nadeau for her beautiful cover artwork and unceasing support.

Jeff Donovick, Dr. Susan Robinson, Dave Greenberg, Dr. David Manson, and Dr. Jonathan Steele, for their education and guidance throughout years of artistic development, as well as their unwavering support in my professional career.

Paul Wilborn, Damon Dougherty, and the Palladium at SPC family for their support…

Sylvia Bertrand, my cherished aunt and godmother, who has been the greatest listener, throughout my life.

Nathan Corder, treasured friend and colleague, for unceasing support, as well as the inspiration to look at the universe and sonic possibilities from differing angles…

My beloved family, friends, and colleagues, who have supported me in my career and life; especially,
Conrhonda Baker, Sanisha Cade, Leo Suarez, Amy O'Dell, Olivia Kieffer, Geneva Stonecipher, Mandy Milliot, William Baker, Robert Fleitz, Sean Hamilton, Eli Ponder-Twardy, Giselle Moraga, and Nikki McShane.

www.ingramcontent.com/pod-product-compliance
Lightning Source LLC
Chambersburg PA
CBHW080635230426
43663CB00016B/2878